On The Street Where You Live

Volume II

Victoria's Early Roads and Railways

On The Street Where You Live

Volume II
Victoria's Early Roads and Railways

Danda Humphreys

Heritage House

This one's for my sister, Jill. The streets we walk along are thousands of miles apart, but she's with me every step of the way.

Copyright © 2000 by Danda Humphreys

CANADIAN CATALOGUING IN PUBLICATION DATA

Humphreys, Danda.
   On the street where you live : Victoria's early roads and railways

   Includes index and bibliography
   ISBN 1-894384-09-1

   1. Roads—British Columbia—Victoria Region—History.
   2. Railroads—British Columiba—Victoria Region—History.
   3. Victoria Region (B.C.)—History.
   I. Title.

FC3846.67.H852 2000   971.1'28   C00-910986-2
F1089.5.V6H84 2000

First edition 2000

   Heritage House acknowledges the financial support of the Government of Canada through the Book Publishing Industry Development Program (BPIDP) for our publishing activities, the British Columbia Arts Council, and the support of the BC Archives.

Front cover: Looking north on Government Street from Fort Street, ca. 1900 (see page 128). Front flap: A Valentine & Sons postcard showing the Parliament Buildings ca. 1910 (top), and a "bird's eye view" of Victoria in 1889 (bottom). Back cover: Two paintings by William George Richardson Hind (1833-1889) showing Victoria's harbour (top) and the Gorge waterway in the 1860s.

Design and layout by Darlene Nickull
Edited by Audrey McClellan

HERITAGE HOUSE PUBLISHING COMPANY LTD.
#108 - 17665 66 A Avenue, Surrey, BC V3S 2A7

Printed in Canada

Canadä

CONTENTS

ACKNOWLEDGEMENTS

*T*his second book about the history of Victoria street names is the direct result of people's continued interest in the history of the city. Some live here now; some lived here in the past; others have only visited. They all share one thing in common— a fascination for the human stories stirred up by street signs.

Many have followed the column called "On The Street Where You Live" in the *Victoria Times Colonist* "Islander" magazine since it started in October 1997. They voted it "the column most read by the most readers" in a reader survey. More than anything else, their positive feedback and enthusiasm have kept me "walking the streets" and ensured the series' continued success.

My thanks to "Islander" editors Peter Salmon and, during Peter's sabbatical, Paul Bennett, for their interest, unfailing support, and lively page layouts.

Thanks also to the many people who write, call, stop me on the street, or e-mail from all over the world. They are quick to voice their appreciation, eager to share stories about their own families, and proud to acknowledge their ancestors' contributions to the growth of Victoria. I am indebted to these people, and to those before them who had the foresight to donate papers, letters, photos, and more to the various archives so that researchers like me could

continue to marvel at the challenges faced by the settlers of long ago.

Archives staff and volunteers work hard to preserve our heritage, and continue to be an invaluable resource for me. Key people include Michael Carter and colleagues (B.C. Archives and Records Service); Bob Griffin (Royal British Columbia Museum); Carey Pallister and Trevor Livelton (Victoria City Archives); Geoff Castle and Jack McIntyre (Saanich Municipal Archives); Lynn Wright (Maritime Museum of British Columbia); Laurette Agnew and members (Saanich Pioneers Society); Peter Barnham and Sherry Eastholm (Sidney Musem); Terry Malone and Elida Pears (Sooke Region Museum and Archives); Daisy Bligh, Ron Bradley, Ron Weir, Ben Swindell, and others (Metchosin School Museum Society). It has been a privilege and a pleasure to work with them all.

Specific help with family and other histories for this volume came from Claire Atkinson (Tatlow); Lorna Thomson Pugh (Sluggett family); Sheila Voaklander (Frank Campbell of "Campbell's Corner"); Bruce Davies of the Craigdarroch Castle Historical Museum Society (Dunsmuir and Weiler families); Bill Blore, Ron Johnstone, and Terry McGinty of the Hatley Park Museum (Dunsmuir family); Brent Wilson, Hayward Thomson, and Irving Funeral Chapel (Hayward family); Eric McMorran (McMorran family); Joan Morison (Fell family);

Brad Morrison (Michell family); Cyl Bethell, Alan and Phyllis Duval, Dorothy Robertson, Frances Robertson, and Norma Sealey (Saanich and Sidney families); Daisy Bligh, Ron Bradley, Ben Swindell, and Ron Weir (Metchosin families); Elida Peers (Sooke families); Karen and Bruce Borden (Simmonds and Borden families, Blenkinsop Valley); Hugh Fraser, Darryl Muralt, Dave Parker, and the B.C. Railways Historical Society (stories about the Victoria & Sidney Railway, British Columbia Electric Railway, and Canadian National Pacific Railway).

Thanks also for information and encouragement from John Adams, Gayle Baird, Jennifer Barr, Maureen Duffus, Chris Hanna, Fred Hook, Caroline Inrig, Jim Munro, Sherri Robinson, and Russ Cameron.

Another tip of the hat to Heritage House for seeing the potential of a second volume of "street stories." Bouquets to Darlene Nickull, whose design helps bring the stories to life. And special thanks to my editor, Audrey McClellan, whose patient organization, questioning mind, and eye for detail ensure that a good read will be had by all.

Last but by no means least, to all the "Islander" readers out there—thanks for sharing my space on Sundays! As always, this book is for you.

INTRODUCTION

Can you remember the name of the street you lived on as a child? I can. Every bend in the road, every gatepost, every crack in the sidewalk is etched in my memory. That street was my life. It led me home. It was so deliciously familiar, I swear that even today I could find my way along it blindfolded.

When you've moved around as much as I have, all those streets start to blur a bit, their names blending together in the great big mixer of time. But some of them stick in my mind. Particularly the first, where I grew up, and the last, where I live now.

How about you? How many times have you wondered about the street where you live…the street you drive along to work…the street you glance at as the bus rolls by? Every street name tells a story. And there is no better place for storytelling than this little bit of heaven on the southern tip of Vancouver Island.

Everyone who has lived in or visited Victoria agrees that there's a sense of history here that isn't found in too many other Canadian cities. Why should that be? The answer lies in its beginnings—the way it was settled. Admittedly, compared to Europe or even the east coast of North America, Victoria's history is short. But what it lacks in length, it makes up for in legend—rich, colourful, and full of surprises. Who could have dreamed, for example, that a place picked out to be just another fur-trading post would one day become a gathering-place for gold miners? Or that a small settlement on a sparsely populated island would one day become the capital of British Columbia?

The area's history dates back many centuries, but European settlement began, to all intents and purposes, with the Hudson's Bay Company's closer exploration of the harbours along this coast. From the moment James Douglas stepped ashore on that spring day in 1842, Victoria's fate was cast. He liked the place. Liked it a lot. Reporting back to Chief Factor John McLoughlin at Fort Vancouver on the Columbia River, Douglas declared that the Port of Camosack was "a perfect Eden in the midst of a dreary northwest wilderness." The following year, he returned with a group of men and set them to work constructing the company's new northern headquarters, henceforth to be known as Fort Victoria.

In Volume One, we watched as the settlement grew from a simple Hudson's Bay fort in a clearing on the east side of the harbour into a bustling township. We listened to the scuffing of boots as thousands of gold miners crowded the dusty streets, gearing up for the Fraser River gold fields where they were convinced a fortune awaited them. And we waited till they returned from those gold fields to celebrate their successes—or drown their sorrows—in one of Victoria's many watering holes.

We looked along today's streets and remembered the key people of those early

Looking north on Wharf Street from opposite the harbour end of today's Bastion Square, the middle of the block houses the offices where Amor de Cosmos launched the first edition of the British Colonist *newspaper on December 11, 1858. In the distance, dense forest around present-day Bay Street marks the outskirts of town.*

days—people whose names continue to crop up in this second volume. We found that Victoria's earliest settlers were a mixture of British, French-Canadian, German, Italian, Jewish, Russian, American, and Chinese … people from all four corners of the world and every walk of life.

Some—like Douglas, Helmcken, Finlayson, Pemberton, Cridge, Thomson, Deans, Begbie, McKenzie and Muir—were recruited by the Hudson's Bay Company; others—like Grant, Blinkhorn, McNeill, Carr, Maynard and Trutch—arrived under their own steam. Some

succeeded, others failed. Some left, others stayed behind. One way or another, every single one of them left their mark.

☞ ☞ ☞ ☞

This book begins on Bastion Street—or more precisely, Bastion Square, once the northern perimeter of Fort Victoria. In the late 1850s the square is the centre of activity—but activity of a different sort than we see there today. Victoria is now a colony, soon to merge with the mainland colony—a move designed to promote

*In the 1890s on Government Street (looking north from Courtney), Victorians
still drive on the left. A southbound streetcar passes a horse and cart
along a street lined with telephone poles and hitching posts.*

growth and protect British interests. The fort is fast disappearing, its bastions, bell-tower, and wooden buildings destined for demolition in favour of commercial buildings.

The Fraser River gold rush has changed everything by introducing other, not always desirable, elements of society into our midst. Victoria's downtown is showing signs of wear and tear as careless newcomers come and go. The HBC elite, anxious to distance themselves until the dust settles, build fine homes on the fringes of the town. Former HBC contract workers, who scattered far and wide to put as many miles as possible between themselves and their former employer, are settled out in the countryside, where hard-working native Indians, Kanakas, and Chinese help them break the land and develop farms.

In 1862, twenty years after James Douglas first set foot on these shores, Victoria is incorporated as a city. Thomas Harris becomes the first mayor. For lack of a better space, city council holds its first meeting in the police barracks alongside the Bastion Street Jail. Council's first job is to clean up the city, stop farm animals wandering freely on the streets, and deal with the drunkenness and disgusting

In the early 1900s, a view from the newly completed Parliament Buildings shows the old, wooden James Bay Bridge replaced by a stone causeway. James Bay has been drained and filled in. Soon the patch of land to the right of the causeway will be home to the magnificent Empress Hotel.

language that bedevil the downtown core. These men are determined that the wayward child called Victoria will grow up to be a beautiful young woman.

Another surge of activity occurs as gold is discovered farther up the Fraser River, in the Cariboo district of the mainland colony of British Columbia. Business in Victoria is booming. Government Street bristles with banks, stores, and saloons. The J.D. Pemberton-designed downtown core expands as people move farther away from it. New streets point long fingers north, south, and east of the city's centre.

Huge tracts of HBC farmland in James Bay and Esquimalt, now subdivided, are criss-crossed by streets named after eastern Canadian cities and lakes, or the people who managed the farms. James Douglas's estate gives its name to the emerging community of Fairfield, which also includes land owned by Isabella Ross. Part of Pemberton's huge estate contains a road called Rockland Avenue, renamed from the less salubrious-sounding Belcher Street at the request of residents. Eastern and southern portions of Oak Bay, once home only to John Tod, the HBC's Uplands Farm, and Captain William McNeill, grow by leaps and bounds as estates are subdivided. Where subdivisions occur at different times, streets don't quite line up, continuing after a dogleg on the far side of what appears to be a T-junction—Davie, Courtney, Ker, and Doncaster are just a few examples of this. Streets like Richardson, Finlayson, and Blenkinsop change their names willy-nilly, to keep us on our toes. Some streets have names that don't seem to make much sense—Ocean View Road is nowhere near the ocean, Broad Street isn't very broad, and View Street doesn't have a view.

As the nineteenth century draws to a close, the clip-clop of horses' hooves gradually gives way to the rumble of rolling stock, as railway lines snake up the Saanich Peninsula. First to start up is the Victoria & Sidney Railway, its cordwood-fed steam engine giving rise to its nickname, "The Cordwood Express". Hot on its heels is the B.C. Electric Railway, which extends its downtown streetcar system to include an interurban line that runs up the west side of the peninsula to Deep Bay (now Deep Cove). And last but not least, the Canadian Northern Pacific Railway connects Patricia Bay with Victoria and the western

communities of Colwood, Metchosin, Sooke, Lake Cowichan, and Youbou. Short-lived though most are, these railways spur unprecedented growth in the previously isolated communities they now serve. They also expand up-Island connections and create a much-needed sea link with the mainland.

From one end of this book to the other, we see Victoria go through enormous changes. Trails and pathways give way to roads and railways. Jitneys and jalopies start to replace horses and carriages. In the Inner Harbour, a causeway connects downtown with the Parliament Buildings and residences in James Bay. The mudflats behind the causeway are gone; in their place rises an elegant hotel. Victoria, the small child with the smudged nose and muddy boots, is becoming a poised and fashionably dressed young woman.

She's followed a fascinating path. Now you can follow it too. Just put on your comfiest walking shoes and take a step back in time. Meet the people Victoria's streets were named after. Marvel at the twists and turns they took along the way. And enjoy this fascinating peek into Victoria's past.

BASTION SQUARE

A gathering of ghosts

*I*n the early 1860s Victoria bore little resemblance to the settlement established by James Douglas, Roderick Finlayson, and Charles Ross. Gone were the palisades and the square, bare buildings of the Hudson's Bay Company fort. Gone was the gate that opened onto the trail leading east through the forest toward Cadboro Bay. Gone were the bastions that for two decades had guarded the HBC workers. All that was left was Bastion Street.

Beginning where the north bastion had once stood, Bastion was a short, stubby street with the city jail at its Langley Street end. The police station and jail had been built in 1858 to provide a focus for law and order and help cope with the scores of lawbreakers who sailed in and out of Victoria in those early gold rush days. Sentencing was swift. The penalty for crime was harsh. The hangman had no mercy. Close to a dozen murderers, miscreants, and other miserable souls, who may or may not have been guilty, breathed their last on the jail yard's gallows. Rumour had it that some of those hanged were buried, not in a cemetery, but beneath the exercise yard on the jail's northeast side.

All this aside, the Victoria of the 1860s was a great, growing place to be. The fortified settlement that for years had been snugly surrounded by Wharf, Government, Bastion, and Broughton streets had spread outward and upward. The government offices had been relocated across the James Bay Bridge, conveniently close to the home of Governor James Douglas. Brick edifices appeared among the wooden, false-fronted, frontier structures. Tradesmen plied their wares. Hotels, brothels, and saloons provided warmth and welcoming smiles. Bastion Street was the very heart of town. It was brassy, bawdy, beery. And it was heaven for a man with a thirst.

There was no shortage of watering holes in and around the square. One of the most popular—the Boomerang Saloon—was owned by a fellow named Ben Griffin. He was an Englishman who had followed the various gold rushes, first to Australia, then to San Francisco, and eventually to Victoria. He and his wife Adelaide weren't interested in mining for gold; they were interested in mining the miners. Business was brisk at the Boomerang. Griffin provided his customers with strong ale, good company, and a generous outpouring of his poems satirizing local personages. Ben was a real character, no doubt about it. But it was Adelaide whose story would become legend long after the Boomerang was gone.

Looking over the top of the courthouse and jail in the 1860s, the heavily treed Esquimalt and Victoria West area can be seen on the other side of what is now the Upper Harbour. The tower behind the courthouse belongs to the firehall on Yates Street.

The dark, square entrance to the Bastion Street Jail (viewed from the middle of today's Bastion Square) must have been a forbidding sight for those whose fate lay in the hands of those who waited inside to judge them.

Bastion Street in the 1860s boasted Macdonald's store (left foreground), the brick courthouse and jail (right background, where the Maritime Museum stands today), and the Boomerang Saloon (toward top left), where saloonkeeper Ben Griffin regaled his patrons with poetry.

Not too long after the Griffins arrived, the young and reasonably robust Adelaide suddenly up and died. She was buried, with due ceremony, in the Quadra Street Burying Ground, with Ben as chief mourner. Surprisingly, considering the shock he must have had, Ben didn't take long to bounce back from the tragedy. He returned to his saloon, resumed regaling patrons with poetry,

and generally seemed to be surviving quite well. At the Boomerang it was "business as usual."

Or was it?

Adelaide appeared to be forgotten—but it seemed she wasn't altogether *gone*. One late evening, as a group of merry miners left the Boomerang to weave their unsteady way home along Langley Street, they were shocked to see the ghostly form of a woman gliding across their path. The apparition was wearing white. It seemed to hover just above the ground. And it bore an uncanny resemblance to Adelaide.

Adelaide was seen many more times, both in the vicinity of the Boomerang and in the Old Burying Ground. Her death was never explained. Ben Griffin died in 1881 at the age of 72. If he held the key to the mystery, he carried it to his grave.

In the late 1880s the city jail was demolished to make way for the towered and turreted courthouse. When the building was officially opened in February 1889, the *Colonist* newspaper reported that "crowds of well and fashionably dressed ladies and gentlemen" picked their way over the muddy streets to attend the celebrations. Among the dignitaries attending was Chief Justice Sir Matthew Baillie Begbie, reported to be standing as tall and as proud as when he had arrived in Victoria 30 years before.

In 1893 the erection of the British Columbia Board of Trade building on the south side of the square caused consternation. It was a skyscraper before the word was known here. It was elegant. It had a tower on the top and the view was outstanding. There was a fine hotel close by. The Law Chambers attracted Victoria's finest legal eagles. And should anyone need it, medical help was at hand—Dr. J.S. Helmcken practised in the building next door.

Over the years, as Victoria grew and the focus of activity moved south and east, Bastion Street lost its splendour. The Victorian buildings faced forlornly onto a public car park. Then in 1965 came a much-needed shot in the arm. Bastion Street became Bastion Square, and its buildings were restored to their former glory.

Today the old courthouse is the Maritime Museum, dominating the east end of a square lined with law offices, pubs, and restaurants. Festivals and folk art adorn the walkway. Flower beds, shrubs, and trees add life to the bricks and stones. The summer sun bathes diners, drinkers, and dalliers in a rosy glow. Music fills the air.

Close your eyes for a moment. Imagine the clattering boots and hearty laughter of the sailors and gold miners and townsfolk swarming eagerly into the street for an evening's entertainment. See the shock on bleary-eyed faces as the lady in white glides by. Hear the anguished scream of the young lad who met his end on the scaffold that once dominated the square.

At night, in the heart of Victoria, the ghosts remain.

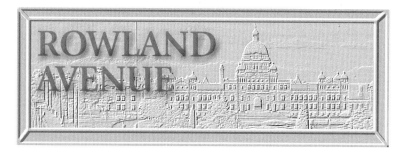

The hangman unmasked

Rowland Avenue is a long way from Bastion Square, but there's a short explanation for the connection between the two. Matthias Rowland was part farmer, part hotelier, and—so the story goes—part hangman at the city jail.

Rowland hailed from Dorsetshire in England. At the age of 30 he left England and sailed around Cape Horn on the HBC's *Norman Morison* with Dr. J.S. Helmcken and more than 50 labourers. They left Gravesend on October 10, 1849. Five months at sea was enough to test the fortitude of any man, and from time to time tempers would flare and a fistfight would result. Helmcken later wrote that Rowland "was the chief boxer, and our butcher too." It was that same scrappy nature that would later lead Helmcken to seek Rowland's assistance at election time. Rowland, he remarked, "could influence half a dozen ignorant people."

After a long, tedious voyage broken by squally seas and an outbreak of smallpox, the *Norman Morison* dropped anchor in Esquimalt on March 24, 1850. Rowland and his shipboard companions gathered their belongings and trudged the muddy three-mile track to Fort Victoria, where their new employer was waiting.

From 1850 to 1854 Rowland was a steward on the paddle-steamer *Beaver* before finishing out his contract as a labourer on dry land. But it was his extracurricular activities, recorded but rarely revealed, that set him apart from other company men. The outgoing, usually voluble Rowland kept his mouth firmly shut about his sinister sideline: hangman for the HBC.

A hangman wears a black hood for a reason; one does not openly gloat about such a grisly occupation. Rowland's identity was kept secret. Records, however, show that he may have officiated at several executions.

One of the first times his services were called for was after the murder of a shepherd stationed at Lake Hill. Peter Brown was shot and killed on a November day in 1852. Governor James Douglas wasted no time or effort in tracking down Brown's attackers. Just two months after the murder, Douglas boarded the *Beaver* and set sail for the Cowichan village where one of the suspects attempted, in vain, to evade capture. The second suspect, a man from the Nanaimo tribe, was caught two weeks later. The two were tried together on the deck of the *Beaver* and hanged at Gallows Point, on Protection Island off Nanaimo, the same day. Records show that the officiating hangman was one Matthias Rowland.

Matthias Rowland (in doorway) is pictured with his family outside his Burnside Hotel, which stood on the north side of Burnside Road at Admirals, just west of today's Pacific Forestry Centre.

This was not Rowland's first hanging; nor, some say, was it his last. Legend has it that some of his later victims met their maker on the gallows in the courtyard of the jail at Bastion Street and are buried there still. A hanging made Rowland richer by ten pounds, which in those days was more than half what the average HBC farm labourer might expect to earn in a whole year.

By 1865, his HBC contract completed, Rowland was settled on the farm he had developed on land he bought in the Burnside area. He later acquired more land from his old shipmate, Dr. Helmcken. At one point his

Burnside Farm covered 500 acres, and Rowland made major contributions to the tax coffers of the town. His land was situated in the area that today includes the Pacific Forestry Centre, Burnside Plaza, and the Town and Country Shopping Centre. The highest section of the acreage is now Rowland Heights subdivision. The farm featured beef cattle and provided dairy products, fruit, and vegetables.

In the late 1800s Rowland ran the Burnside Hotel, which stood on the north side of Burnside and Admirals Road. With the naval base at Esquimalt not too far south, and precious

One of the barns on Rowland's farm stood where Burnside Plaza is today. His property included the land now covered by Tillicum Mall and Town and Country Shopping Centre.

few other watering holes around, the hotel did a roaring trade. Rowland prospered as a hotelier in the same way that he had prospered as a farmer: through a mixture of ambition and hard work. He was a frugal fellow and not inclined to spend unnecessarily. In 1879, when a bay colt wandered onto his property, Rowland advertised its presence in the *Colonist* and offered to return the colt to its rightful owner provided the owner agreed to foot the bill for the ad.

Matthias and his English-born wife Eliza raised several daughters and a son. The children attended the nearby Craigflower School. Most of them married and remained in the area. Eliza died in 1899 of a cerebral haemorrhage. Four years later Matthias died as a result of chronic bronchitis. He was buried beside Eliza at Ross Bay Cemetery on January 28, 1903.

His Last Will and Testament, dated March 1900, describes Rowland as a "Farmer and Hotel Proprietor." There is no mention anywhere, except in colonial account books, of his other, unrecognized occupation. Rowland Avenue, a dead-end street that runs parallel to Carey Road, is the only reminder of the HBC hangman who once called this area home.

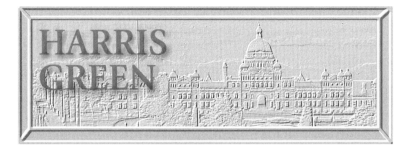

Mayor a man of meats

Matthias Rowland may have been the butcher aboard the *Norman Morison* in 1849, but the first man to open a butcher shop on Vancouver Island was Thomas Harris.

Harris was a farmer's son, born in Hertfordshire, England, in 1817. By the 1840s he was in business for himself in Liverpool. While there he married Mrs. Dickinson, a widow with three sons. Two daughters were born shortly after.

In 1854, when youngest daughter Emily was three years old, Harris moved his family to San Francisco. Four years later, with visions of a secure future feeding hungry gold miners, the Harrises set sail for Victoria.

By June 1858, with the population of the town swelling daily, the Queen's Meat Market on the corner of Government and Johnson streets was doing a roaring trade. Orders from households, hotels, and restaurants kept the staff busy and Harris in pocket. Before long he was able to build a fine home for his family at the northwest corner of Bastion and Government streets. It was a brick edifice, splendid for its time, with a grilled balcony and fine lines that caused it to stand out from the simpler buildings surrounding it.

Little by little, Harris involved himself in various public activities in the town. He liked to describe himself as " just an 'umble tradesman," but humble he certainly was not. Nor was he ever short of an opinion or likely to back down from an argument. What he lacked in formal education

Mr. and Mrs. Thomas Harris

*Looking north along Government Street from Fort Street in the late 1860s,
Harris's building can be seen at left of the water cart, in the centre of the photo.*

he made up for in firmness and sheer physical presence. Bald of head and florid of face, he was a veritable giant of a man, with an ego to match.

In early 1862, having dabbled in everything from business ventures to real estate to shipping, Harris was ready to dabble in politics. In March of that year he was elected member of the legislative assembly for Esquimalt Town district, though he didn't hold his seat for long. By August he had thrown his hat into the ring for the position of mayor of Victoria. He was 46 years old.

Victoria was growing by leaps and bounds. In just two years it had sprouted a new timber bridge across James Bay, purpose-built government offices, macadamized streets, hotels, a jail, a fire hall, five churches, a theatre, schools, and a hospital. The 1863 City Directory boasted regular steamship service between Victoria and San Francisco. Chief exports were coal, lumber, furs and skins, fish, and fish oil. The upsurge in commercial and residential development spurred Victoria's incorporation as a city. On August 2, 1862, Governor James Douglas signed the Act of Incorporation in the legislature, and the business of electing a mayor and councillors began.

As elections go, this one was nothing if not straightforward. There was a candidates' meeting on August 12, and the first municipal election day was August 16, 1862. About 600 people gathered—only the men with money or land. There was no secret ballot and only two candidates for mayor. Voting was by a show of hands—a few for Alfred Waddington; a veritable forest for Harris. Amid wild excitement and most vociferous cheering, Thomas Harris was elected first mayor of Victoria. On August 18, six councillors were elected, and on August 25, 1862, Victoria City Council met for the first time, in the police barracks alongside the county jail.

Harris leased the lower floor of his family home on the northwest corner of Government and Bastion Streets to the Bank of British Columbia. It was later replaced by the Bank of Montreal building, which still stands (though it no longer houses a bank) on the same site.

It was the second council meeting that cemented Harris's reputation for weighty discourse. One minute he was looking over the judge's bench; the next he had disappeared behind it. First his bald head appeared, then his red and rather serious face. It became apparent that the armchair provided had collapsed beneath his 300-plus-pound weight, and Victoria's top man in town had been unceremoniously dumped on the floor. He had alighted, said His Worship, on that portion of his breeches which wears out first.

Quickly the council turned its attention to more serious matters, striking a Committee on Nuisances to decide which of the city's many problems should be dealt with first. The stench of stagnant water on Yates Street, pesky pigs that wandered the downtown core, and drunkenness and disgusting language on Humboldt Street vied for the council's attention alongside bawdy houses and brothels.

Council wasted no time. By September the word was out: straying pigs and goats would be impounded; the firing of guns and pistols in the city would not be tolerated; horse-drawn traffic was to keep to the left-hand side of the road with a travelling speed not exceeding eight miles per hour. It was a start.

Harris worked hard and played hard. He was known for his love of good food, good wine, and horse racing and was never happier than when thundering around Beacon Hill Park's rough racetrack on his favourite mount, George. He was a competent as well as a jovial jockey, winning almost every race he entered.

Unfortunately he didn't fare as well in the council chamber. In 1863 he defeated his opponent by a much narrower margin, and in 1864 decided to retire from civic politics.

All was not going well on the financial front either. Having spent his money faster than he could comfortably make it, Harris had leased the lower floor of his residence to the newly arrived Bank of British Columbia and moved his family to a more modest home nearby.

Then came a further blow. While riding out on West Saanich Road he fell from his buggy, sustaining fractures to an arm and a leg. He never regained full use of his limbs. Nevertheless, he continued to be politically active. He became legislative sergeant-at-arms, sought election to the House of Commons, and was high sheriff of Victoria when he died, at the age of 68, in 1884.

Bishop Edward Cridge officiated at the funeral service at the Reformed Episcopal Church. The mayor and members of council, civic officers, police officers, and firemen followed behind Harris's widow and children as the procession made its way to Ross Bay Cemetery, where Victoria's first mayor was laid to rest. Thomas Harris is remembered in Harris Island and Mayor Channel off the southeast coast of Vancouver Island (Emily Islet commemorates his youngest daughter). In Victoria, only a wooden marker on a green roadside strip along Pandora Street reminds us of this larger-than-life character.

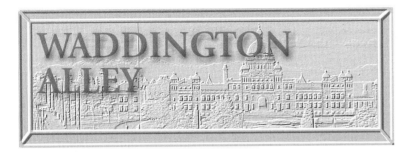

Champion of lost causes

A short distance west of Thomas Harris's butcher shop, another recent arrival was making money from the gold miners on the streets surrounding Fort Victoria. Before long, both newcomers would be nominated for the top position in town. Harris became first mayor of Victoria, but his opponent also won a place in the history of B.C.

Alfred Penderill Waddington was born in London in 1801, the tenth child and sixth son of a wealthy Nottinghamshire land-owner. His distinguished ancestry, divided between England and France, traced back to the twelfth century. Waddington was seven-teen when his father died, and he joined his older brother in France. Two years of business education in Paris were followed by two years' university education in Germany. Despite this, his business dealings were far from successful. In the 1840s, lighter of pocket and looking for adventure, he set sail for British North America.

In 1850 Waddington followed the gold rush to California. Once in San Francisco,

Alfred Waddington

commercial opportunities beckoned. By 1854 he was in partnership with a Frenchman. Dulip and Waddington imported fine French and English groceries and wines. Business was brisk; so brisk that when gold rush fever spread north a few years later, Waddington followed along to Victoria.

It was April 1858. He was enchanted by the peaceful settlement with its smattering of grass-covered streets—and shocked when the peace was suddenly shattered by the shouts of hungry gold miners. Not that he wasn't ready for them; he had purchased several parcels of land from the Hudson's Bay Company with just such an invasion in mind. To increase his options he had even cut a path through the middle of his three adjacent lots between Yates and Johnson streets, creating a short, narrow lane that quickly became home to entrepreneurial activities that included a butcher's, a baker's, and a bowling alley. The stage was set for financial success.

By the fall, however, everything had changed. Disappointed miners, finding no fortune on the Fraser, were leaving as fast as they

Looking down Waddington's Alley from Johnson Street to Yates Street in the 1890s, with Morley's Soda Water Factory in the left foreground.

had arrived. Hotel rooms were empty; saloons were silent; product lay unpurchased on storekeepers' shelves.

Waddington was appalled. Quickly he produced the colony's first non-government publication, a book entitled *The Fraser Mines Vindicated*, and an inaccurate but immensely popular map to show miners the road to golden opportunity.

Inspired by the businesslike environment south of the border, and infuriated by what he saw as the HBC's foolish pursuit of frivolity, Waddington railed against the company. In a letter to the editor he wrote, "On the American side they have lighthouses where wanted; buoys where wanted; roads and communications; but they have no admirals, no brilliant officers, no high-society balls. On the English side, we have all the latter." He was strongly opposed to the HBC's domination of local activities and felt that Douglas's autocratic rule was hindering full development of the colony.

It wasn't that he was anti-HBC. In his book he paid the company many compliments, but he ended his praise of early HBC activities in the area with the observation, "But now that a more enlightened population has taken possession of the country, the object of the company for the purpose of civilization is at an end, and its intervention for commercial purposes a nuisance." It was time, he said, for a change to a more democratic form of government. The citizens, impressed by the eloquence and conviction of this short, stocky Englishman, responded by electing him to the legislative assembly for Victoria District.

It wasn't really his cup of tea. He turned up late for most meetings; many other members didn't turn up at all. Inevitably it was

Homathko River in Waddington Canyon was the scene of a horrific massacre in 1864, when fourteen workers on Waddington's road project were killed in retaliation for provoking the local Chilcotin people.

the arrival of "Old Waddy"—he was now 57—that signalled a quorum, when business could finally begin. He became a champion of lost causes, an outspoken critic of autocratic rule, and a prolific writer.

The gold find in the North Fraser galvanized him into action. Convinced that the best route to the Cariboo was from the coast, he persuaded Governor James Douglas to give him permission to build a wagon road from the head of Bute Inlet to Fort Alexandria. He would finance construction, he said, in return for being allowed to collect tolls on completion. Waddington resigned from the legislature so he could focus his energies on this new enterprise. Work started in the spring of 1862, and by the end of that year, 53 kilometres of

road had been built, along with a total of 66 bridges over the Homathko River.

It was an impressive beginning. However, workers returning to the area in the spring of 1863 found the bridges had been washed away. Every single one had to be repaired or replaced before work could continue. Then came another devastating blow. In April 1864, senseless provocation of a group of Chilcotin men resulted in the massacre of fourteen out of seventeen members of a working party in the Homathko Canyon.

Six Chilcotin men were arrested, charged with the murders, and sentenced to hang by Judge Matthew Baillie Begbie. But it was too late. Waddington had already disposed of his Victoria property to provide continued financing for the project. Now his funds were almost depleted and he was forced to admit defeat.

In June 1865 he accepted the offer of a position as superintendent of schools for Vancouver Island. Although he performed his duties with diligence, he found them confining and uninspiring. When the Lower Mainland and Vancouver Island colonies combined in 1866, he resigned his position.

Waddington was more than ever convinced of the value of an overland route that started on the coast. When the idea of a cross-continental railroad came up during discussions of Confederation, he proposed the Bute Inlet area as its western terminus. A carefully designed combination of tramways, steamers, and a wagon road, he said, could effectively connect B.C. with Edmonton and points east, thus promoting trade in the North Pacific.

In 1867 he travelled to England at his own expense to negotiate financing for the project.

He was delighted at the support his ideas received. Success was within reach; he was convinced that he would recover all the money he had lost. When Burrard Inlet was declared the western terminus for the railroad, Waddington swallowed his disappointment and suggested that a bridge and two ferries could provide the needed link with Vancouver Island.

But success eluded him still. In Ottawa in February 1872 he contracted smallpox and was dead within two weeks. Single, single-minded, and 70 years old, he was buried in St. James Cemetery, Hull, Quebec.

The man whom journalist D.W. Higgins once described as a fellow with "a noble, generous heart ... a fine old English gentleman," had crossed his last hurdle. A lifelong bachelor, he left no family to mourn him. Only a mainland mountain and harbour and a narrow Victoria street remind us of his name.

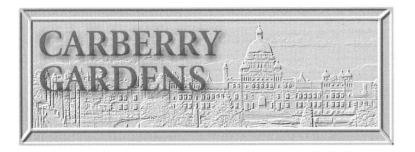

Breadmaker couldn't crack the upper crust

*F*rom his bakery east of Waddington's alley and south of Harris's butcher shop, Samuel Nesbitt provided the town with the basic food of life. As long as men had appetites, his product would never go out of style. When gold rush fever spread north, hungry miners followed the smell of freshly baked bread right to Nesbitt's door.

Like Waddington, Samuel Nesbitt arrived in Victoria via California. Unlike Waddington, however, he made money there. Still in his twenties when he moved to Vancouver Island in 1858, he carried enough American gold coin to buy a piece of Dr. J.S. Helmcken's land on Yates Street near Broad. He started a bread-baking business— Victoria's first commercial bakery. It was a winner. Life was good. Good enough that when the bride ship *Tynemouth* sailed into Esquimalt four years later, Nesbitt was ready to take a bride.

His wife was one of many single females sent from England in answer to Reverend Edward Cridge's cry for help. The men of Victoria, said

Cridge, needed women to partner them. The B.C. Emigration Society in England obliged with a boatload of young ladies marked for marriage to the men of this town.

The *Tynemouth* left England in the spring of 1862. By September 17 it had reached its destination. The passengers disembarked. One among them— eighteen-year-old Jane Anne Saunders—took Nesbitt's fancy. The handsome young Irishman and the London girl were wed seven months later, in the spring of 1863. They lived in a house they called "Holly Lodge," on Cormorant Street near Quadra, a few short blocks from the bakery. Several children were born to the couple, but most were weak and sickly and didn't survive.

Samuel Nesbitt

Nesbitt's business, by contrast, went from strength to strength. Before he arrived, the women of Victoria had to buy baked goods from the nearest supplier at Port Townsend or make their own. A local supply of fresh bread was a novelty, and the ladies loved it. Local merchants were supportive—buying Nesbitt's bread cost

A six-foot-deep second-floor balcony afforded views in all directions from Nesbitt's $10,000 "Erin Hall." Society snobs called it "Cracker Castle" because it was built with the profits from Nesbitt's biscuit company.

less than importing it from Port Townsend. Nesbitt didn't need to follow the gold rush to the Fraser. As long as the dough kept rising, his bank balance would rise along with it.

When he outgrew his original premises, he moved his business to the western end of Fort Street and installed newer, more powerful machinery. Before long he obtained a valuable contract to provide bread and biscuits to the Navy and built another bakery on the Esquimalt Dock. Its proximity to the water eased the loading of bread and biscuits onto naval vessels—and precipitated its downfall. One day early in 1867 the dock collapsed, and Nesbitt's bakery slid slowly into the briny. Undeterred, he quickly built another, this time on more solid ground.

By now it was time for his family to move

from the downtown area. Nesbitt found a patch of land that suited him. No matter that it was out in the country and a trifle isolated; the ten-acre parcel on Cadboro Bay Road, as that part of Fort Street was then called, was the perfect spot for a fine new home. Designed to resemble a typical manor house in his native Ireland, Nesbitt's "Erin Hall" cost $10,000 to build and was much admired when it was completed in 1874. The *Colonist* described it as "commodious, elegant and costly." Indeed, it was a splendid edifice and worthy of the man who made his money putting bread on townsfolk's tables.

Nesbitt had learned the value of a good foundation. "Erin Hall" had one of solid rock. It was surrounded by formal gardens, orchards, and wild-flowered woods. A curving driveway, now called Carberry Gardens, connected it with Cadboro Bay Road. The six-foot-deep balcony surrounding the house afforded a magnificent, 360-degree view.

On the first floor of the home, double parlours, a breakfast room, and a dining room shared space with a library, kitchen, bathroom, and offices. A handsome black walnut staircase led to five large, thirteen-foot-ceilinged bedrooms on the second floor. It was, to say the least, an imposing dwelling, standing like an exclamation point atop the hill leading east from the town. With the sweat of his brow and the stroke of an architect's pen, Nesbitt had made his mark. He was ready to move in more salubrious social circles.

But the baker's efforts barely curled the edges of Victoria's upper crust. He was, after all, still just a tradesman. Compared to fellow-countrymen Joseph Pemberton, Victoria's town planner, and Judge Peter O'Reilly, both raised in well-established Irish families, Nesbitt was "low born." Early in his career he had been president of Victoria's first labour organization,

the Practical Baker's Association. He had married a "bride-ship bride." And to cap it all, his home had been built with the proceeds of a bread-and-biscuit business. He called it "Erin Hall"; the society snobs called it "Cracker Castle."

None of this seemed to concern Nesbitt. He thrived in his new environment. But he didn't live to enjoy it for long. In the early spring of 1881 he developed what the *Colonist* described as "a wasting illness." Two months later, barely into his fifth decade, he was dead. Bishop Cridge conducted the funeral service, and he was buried at Ross Bay Cemetery.

With the help of eldest son Sam, Jane took over the Fort Street bakery and turned it into a $30,000-a-year business. In later life she travelled extensively, and in 1897, at the age of 54, she died and was buried beside her husband.

One hundred years after Jane stepped ashore at Esquimalt, "Erin Hall" burned down. All that remains of this enterprising pair is a white marble mantel in a house on Pemberton Road and grandson James K. Nesbitt's wonderful written legacy of Victoria's early years.

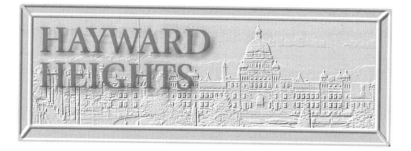

HAYWARD HEIGHTS

Carpenter served citizens from the cradle to the grave

*I*n the early 1860s, a short walk along Wharf Street from Nesbitt's bakery would lead you to the business premises of a fellow who figured largely in the final days of Victoria's early residents. Charles Hayward, first undertaker in the city, prepared Nesbitt and many other pioneers for the journey to their final resting place.

Charles Hayward, oldest son of a Stratford, Essex, merchant, was born in 1839. At the age of fourteen he apprenticed as a carpenter and joiner and spent seven years perfecting his trade. But work was hard to come by and competition was fierce. Hayward was an ambitious young fellow. He became convinced that his prospects in England paled in comparison to the glitter of gold in a new land far away.

Three days after he married sweetheart Sarah McChesney in London, Charles travelled to Southampton and boarded the *Shannon*, bound for Panama. It was March 1862. He was just 22 years old.

Sadness at leaving home and family behind was quickly replaced by delight in this new

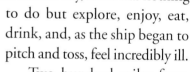

Charles Hayward

adventure. Cramped quarters and the noise of the paddles destroyed his sleep but didn't dampen his enthusiasm. He was on his way, and each meal bell promised good food and good company. As the *Shannon* moved out into the open ocean on the second day, there was nothing to do but explore, enjoy, eat, drink, and, as the ship began to pitch and toss, feel incredibly ill.

Two hundred miles from land, meal bells had long since lost their charm. Stomachs churned at the news that, in preparation for the next meal, the butcher had dispatched a pig with a blow from his mallet. No one felt like food; they were all too busy "feeding the fishes." After two miserable days, Hayward, a devout teetotaller, was persuaded to take a dose of brandy—and to his amazement, immediately began to feel better.

Now he could enjoy the beautiful sunsets and, once the sun had disappeared below the horizon, the clarity of the constellations. His own bright star in England was never far from his mind; he wondered if she was enjoying the same sight. Then three things happened in fairly quick succession. Clear weather gave way to storms that drowned four of the remaining pigs in the hold. A seemingly healthy man died of smallpox. And about two-thirds of the way between England and Panama, Hayward started to have second thoughts about his future.

His shipmates on the *Shannon* spoke confidently of the success they expected to experience at the gold fields. Listening to them, Hayward wasn't so sure that he was cut out to be a gold miner after all. "There is something disreputable about goldmining," he wrote in his diary. Deciding that "a good name is better than riches," he vowed that when he reached his new home he would forget about prospecting and pursue his chosen trade.

At St. Thomas in the Virgin Islands, Hayward was fascinated by the "darkies" who swarmed around the *Shannon* in their frail boats, waiting to take its passengers ashore. He and his companions transferred to a smaller, severely overloaded ship. As well as its human cargo, the *Tamar* carried cockroaches, and the travellers were relieved when its five-day voyage was over.

They took a train across the Isthmus of Panama. Hayward was shocked by the poverty he noted along the single-line track and awed by the sight of dense forests filled with panthers, alligators, and crocodiles. The three-hour train journey was exhausting, and an overnight stay in Panama City was appreciated.

The next day they boarded the *Sonora* and set off for San Francisco. Work was well paid there, but people were rough, and Hayward felt that certain groups of immigrants were treated poorly. It was a far cry from the safe, sheltered life he had left behind. "I do not like Americans," he confided to his diary, and gratefully embarked on the last leg of his journey.

The journey north via Astoria and Portland was breathtaking in its beauty, but the *Sierra Nevada* carried far too many passengers and, like many others, Hayward was obliged to sleep on deck. Daily divine services helped raise his spirits, but by the time the ship reached Esquimalt in May 1862, he'd had more than enough of the sea.

Stepping ashore in late spring, he did not care that the sidewalks were planked and the roads were dusty, destined to turn to mud in wet weather. He saw a small town with the remnants of a fort still standing and a population of some 10,000 people, many of them permanent residents. Surely someone with his skills would be welcome here.

But work proved hard to find. Hayward was glad to meet Reverend Cridge, an old friend of his family's, and obtain a letter of introduction to the Hudson's Bay Company's accountant, Roderick Finlayson. He was often tempted to travel farther afield, but the tales told by shipmates from the *Shannon* who had returned from the Fraser River convinced Hayward he should stay put.

In these worrisome days he missed his young wife terribly and constantly chastised himself for leaving her behind. "I wish dear Sarah was coming in the next vessel," he wrote. Slowly but surely, however, carpentering work trickled in, and before long he was able to start a sash-and-door business and send for his beloved Sarah. In the third week of October he learned she was on her way.

By the beginning of November his diary records a heady mix of passion, piety, and practicality. "I am almost mad with delight at the thought of soon meeting my precious jewel again. Heavenly Father be pleased to smile upon

Hayward's ornate, silver-trimmed hearse is pictured here outside his sash-and-door factory at Langley and Broughton streets. Black-plumed and draped horses pulled the hearse slowly along the funeral route. Pedestrians stood silently out of respect while the funeral procession passed by.

her and bring her safely to the haven where she would be. Am busy making a bedstead."

There was disappointment when the *Robert Lowe* failed to arrive, as expected, by Christmas. And there was dismay when news broke of a vessel wrecked off Race Rocks. Not content with assurances that no such wreck had taken place, Hayward climbed Beacon Hill to satisfy himself that Sarah was not in danger.

Eventually his prayers were answered. On January 10, 1863, her ship sailed into harbour. They were together at last.

With Sarah by his side, Hayward took a new lease on life. No more sleeping on the floor with his boots for a pillow. No more lonely nights. His home was furnished, it was comfortable, and it was filled with love.

Work was plentiful. Soon Hayward's sash-and-door factory on Broughton Street was supplied with materials from his own steam sawmill on Langley Street. It was a small step from cabinets to caskets, and in 1867 he established Victoria's first funeral parlour on the west side of Government Street, between Fort and Courtney.

At Hayward's B.C. Funeral Furnishing Co., clients could choose between traditional wood or specially imported metallic burial caskets and several different kinds of burial robes. Hayward gave thanks to his Lord for helping him resist the tempting glitter of gold. Like biscuit-maker Nesbitt on the other end of the block, he had found a recipe for success. Dying followed living as surely as night followed day. The funeral business would never go out of style.

Happy in their new home on Fort Street, Sarah produced the first of their nine children. A few years later when triplets arrived—the first born to a white woman in this province—Sarah received three guineas from Queen Victoria for her pains. Only one of the triplets, a girl, survived. Then deadly diphtheria hit the family hard. Six of their children didn't live to see the turn of the century.

Hayward's first foray into politics, in 1873, was a firm foundation for a lifetime of community service. As a member of city council he was largely responsible for development of the waterworks that eventually eliminated the need for barrels of water to be transported downtown from Spring Ridge by horse and cart. Sarah was a teacher, then principal at a girls' school, and was involved in charitable causes.

Charles moved his business to larger premises on the north side of Broughton, between Douglas and Blanshard. In 1885 he also moved his family from a house at 1013 Vancouver Street to a grand new Italianate villa on the lot next door, at a cost of $6,000.

Forty-six-year-old Hayward cut quite a figure. Tall, sedate, and bearded, he was always well groomed and often seen in a morning coat, as befitted a man of his calling. His motto—"Any job worth doing is worth undertaking"—reflected his responsible, hard-working outlook on life. A true Christian gentleman, he rarely missed a Sunday sermon at the church he had helped build in 1875 at the foot of Blanshard Street for his friend Bishop Cridge. Over the years he was a member of the city council, a member of the Pacific Club, director of the Royal Jubilee Hospital, president of the B.C. Protestant Orphanage, secretary and then chair of the school board, and chief magistrate.

In 1899 Hayward became mayor for the first of three terms. Among his many accomplishments was the replacement of the rickety old James Bay Bridge with a solid causeway that linked James Bay and the busy downtown area.

By the 1890s, when this picture was taken, Hayward's B.C. Funeral Furnishing Co. had relocated to the north side of Broughton Street, between Douglas and Blanshard. His own funeral was conducted from here in 1919. The business he founded continues in Victoria to this day.

When this was completed, the city was able to enter into an agreement with the CPR to build a hotel on a portion of the newly drained James Bay mudflats. He also managed to consolidate the city's debt.

As the 1800s drew to a close, business was booming and Hayward's funerals were a sight to behold. Matched black horses, plumed and draped in black from one end to the other, pulled black hearses decorated with ornate carvings, silver trim, and plate glass. There was no relief from summer insects for the poor beasts of burden; their natural fly swatters were flattened by black, tassel-decorated net. Children's funerals featured white ponies draped in white. In those slower, more respectful times, everything stopped for the solemn procession with its visible symbols of grief.

Some funeral arrangements proved more challenging than others. Maritime disasters were all too common. One of the worst was the sinking of the *Valencia*, en route from San Francisco in January 1906. The ship missed the entrance to the Strait of Juan de Fuca and crashed onto the rocks at Pachena Point. Three-quarters of the passengers and crew were lost—about 117 people. Bodies were tossed by the waves and torn by rocks and gravel. By the time they were recovered, most were unrecognizable. With no papers or possessions to provide clues, Hayward was forced to bury the unidentified remains.

In an attempt to notify families, he placed ads in newspapers all across North America. His descriptions of the bodies were as detailed as he could make them. Body No. 12 was a woman, apparently young, her face damaged beyond description, wearing a gold chain bracelet with a small padlock and one Oxford tie shoe. Body No. 14 was a heavy-limbed boy, aged about sixteen, with gold crowns on his teeth and brown socks. Body No. 15 wore a white shirt with a

white Cluett & Peabody-stamped collar, size 8 patent leather footwear, and a tattoo on his left arm that featured an eagle above the U.S. flag. One by one the pitiful remains were described in print. Hayward's meticulous attention to detail resulted in identification of many of the victims. Because of his efforts, the bodies could be exhumed and shipped to bereaved relatives for burial closer to home.

The sinking of the *Valencia* marked Hayward's fifth year as a widower. During his second term as mayor, in 1901, Sarah had died of heart disease. She was 61. Flags flew at half-mast in recognition of her many contributions to the community.

Eighteen years later, Charles died of cancer in his 80th year. The director of hundreds of funerals for others was now the centre of his own. It was a splendid affair, one of the largest funerals ever held in Victoria. The procession moved slowly to Ross Bay Cemetery, where the carpenter-turned-undertaker was buried beside his wife.

The Haywards are remembered in Hayward Heights, off Kings Road just east of Cook Street, and in the house Charles built for his family in 1885 on the northeast corner of Vancouver and Rockland streets. A handsome heritage home, it stands to this day as a monument to one man's faith and the funeral company that still bears his name.

FELL STREET

From grocer to mayor with flair

About the time Charles Hayward was arriving in Victoria, another Englishman who would later be mayor was setting off on his own voyage to North America.

James Fell was born in 1821 on a farm at Muncaster Head, Cumberland, on England's northwest coast. He was the son of James Fell and Jane Johnston. James Senior was manager of the home farm that supplied produce for General Sir Henry Wyndham at Cockermouth. At age fifteen, James Junior apprenticed as a grocer. He went to London for a year to learn about tea importing, and went on to develop his own general grocery business.

James Fell

In 1849, at the age of 28, he married 30-year-old Sarah Thornton in Liverpool. They had five children—Martha, James Frederic (known as Fred), Thornton, Jessie, and Marion. Another son, Frank, died as a baby. Sarah caught a chill after youngest son Wilfred's December 1862 birth and died on Christmas Day. Wilfred died eight weeks later.

Before Wilfred's birth, in May 1862, James and eight-year-old Fred had left England to try their luck at gold mining in that new land far across the sea. They travelled through Mexico and California and arrived in Victoria in July, where they camped for about six days on a spot between the present Point Ellice and Rock Bay bridges while they geared up. Then they boarded the schooner *North Star* with other gold seekers bound for the Cariboo.

It was a far from positive experience. On July 31 Fell felt obliged to write a letter to the editor of the *Colonist*. He claimed that the possibilities of finding gold in the Cariboo were over-exaggerated, warned of the disappointment experienced by many of those seeking a fortune, and suggested that others think twice before journeying there.

By spring he was back in Victoria, facing life without his beloved Sarah.

Buoyed by an independent, entrepreneurial spirit, he opened a grocery store on Broad Street.

Fell stayed on at his View Street home until his death in 1890.

Investing his money wisely, he soon bought a bigger shop, and in 1877 he bought land and erected a building at the corner of Fort and Broad streets, which stands to this day.

This was an era when men did the grocery shopping. Many a potential purchaser of foodstuffs would be enticed to Fell's shop by the pungent aroma of coffee and spices and the promise of lively conversation. A convivial person and never short of an opinion, Fell was always entertaining to be around. A quick stop at Grocer Fell's for a wee drop and a chat could well turn into an afternoon of animated discourse.

His home life was no less fulfilling. Still a widower, he lived on View Street between Cook and Ormond. Fred and his wife lived at the corner of Pandora and Cook. Three other children had joined him in Victoria. Thornton and his wife lived up on Fort Street, while Jessie and Marion and their families were just around the corner.

Fell was a generous fellow, known for his civic-mindedness and his involvement with societies and benevolent associations. Twice elected to the position of chief magistrate, he was a member of the school board and was a trustee of Jubilee Hospital. He helped fund the Mechanics Institute and put up $400 for Victoria's first free library. Always ready to help others who needed a financial hand, he was at the mercy of many a money-hungry malingerer. Many years later his survivors found bundles of unpaid IOUs from people whose business ventures he'd agreed to bankroll.

A political animal at heart, Fell decided to run for mayor in 1863. He lost. In 1882 he ran for the House of Commons but was not elected. Nothing if not persistent, he ran for mayor again in 1885 and won. He immediately turned council's attention toward such matters as a sewage system, the impending visit of Prime Minister Sir John A. Macdonald to pound home

Fell & Co. Grocery stood proudly at the southeast corner of Fort and Broad streets, in a building that is still called the Fell Block to this day.

the last spike on the Esquimalt & Nanaimo (E&N) Railway line, and the soon-to-be-celebrated Golden Jubilee of Queen Victoria.

Fell was, without a doubt, one of Victoria's more colourful politicians and certainly one of the most rotund. His trademarks were a top hat and a gold watch chain stretched across his ample front. Council meetings were lively. Fell loved a good argument, and when given the floor he was not above rhapsodizing to the point of exhaustion. But enough was enough. When faced with a third term as mayor in 1887, he decided to retire.

Around this same time, the ever-curious Fell became interested in spiritualism. Still faithful to the memory of his beloved Sarah, he joined the Spiritualist Society, a group that regularly attempted to communicate with the dead. Fell became president of the Society, whose members included David Higgins, erstwhile editor of the *Colonist*, who lived just a few blocks away, and pioneer photographer Hannah Maynard.

Always attracted to the unusual and unconventional, Fell became a fervent supporter of a newcomer to town. Mrs. Henry Lake had startled staid Victorians with her talk of birth control and free love. An editorial in the *Colonist* decried her views, but Fell defended them and became, in the process, one of the earliest and most energetic local supporters of women's issues. His enthusiastic involvements, it seemed, knew no bounds.

But in November 1890 his excess weight, love of liquor, and family history of heart disease finally began to catch up with him. Gradually he started to fail. On December 8, 1890, he died at his View Street home. Members of the St. George's Society, the Odd Fellows, other benevolent societies, and the Board of Trade attended his funeral. A long, solemn procession wound its way to Ross Bay Cemetery, where the English grocer who became one of Victoria's many memorable mayors was finally laid to rest.

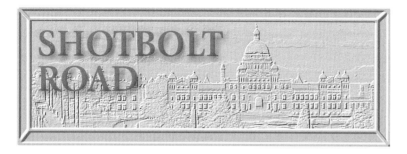

SHOTBOLT ROAD

Pills and potions for pioneers

*I*f patrons tired of the talk at Fell's Grocery, they didn't have far to go for a new angle on any subject. A few blocks north, at Shotbolt's Pharmacy, another group would doubtless be debating politics, the gold rush in the Cariboo, or the newly discovered find on the Leech River near Sooke. Thomas Shotbolt, like James Fell, delighted in providing a venue where the issues of the day could be freely discussed.

Shotbolt was born in Lincolnshire, England, in 1842. He apprenticed as a druggist in Horncastle, Lincolnshire, at the age of fifteen, obtaining his chemist and druggist diploma when he was twenty.

Thomas and Lavinia Shotbolt

By then, news of the gold strike in the Cariboo had reached the old country, and Shotbolt determined to try his luck. Sailing from England to Panama and then to San Francisco, he boarded the *Sierra Nevada*.

By July 1862 Shotbolt had reached his new home. Working at first with another druggist, he established his own business a few weeks later on the south side of Johnson Street, just west of Government. Determined to adhere to high English standards, he stocked only the purest, freshest drugs imported directly from England and the Continent.

So wrapped up was he in his business that it was twelve years before he began to think seriously of taking a wife. In May 1875 he married Lavinia Parmiter in the iron Anglican church, St. John's, and took her to live in modest quarters above the pharmacy. Two years later he purchased the lot and built a brick structure on the site of the old store. His new store had polished counters, high ceilings, and plentiful lighting. It contained an impressive array of goods, with more housed in a two-storey brick

Shotbolt's pharmacy sold choice products imported directly from England and the Continent. A five-room suite on the second floor housed his growing family. The building, minus its second floor, stands to this day on the south side of Johnson Street, just west of Government.

a later owner of the store kept rows of ancient bottles, magnificent blue stone ointment and pill jars, and Shotbolt's original iron mortar and pestle on display to delight visitors.

The downtown area was becoming more crowded and less desirable, so in the mid-1880s Shotbolt had a beautiful three-storey house built at 1901 Fairfield Road. "Hollywood" was at the centre of a ten-acre property on the western slope of Gonzales Hill. A carriageway wound up from the stone-pillared iron gate to the stables at the back of the house. A conservatory on the south aspect had purple, amber, and mauve-paned bay windows. The drawing room boasted gilt mouldings and a frescoed ceiling that supported a chandelier. Arches by the windows had cupid's faces at either end. An artistic newel post graced the fine staircase, and a coloured glass window lighted the landing, while a lookout tower afforded a magnificent view of Race Rocks and the Inner Harbour.

Behind the house was a hill that begged to be climbed, and not far away a beach stretched invitingly. It was the perfect environment for the Shotbolts' four children. Lavinia, too, was in her element. After years of patiently cultivating geraniums and chrysanthemums in tubs on the back porch at dusty Johnson Street, she now had the luxury of a real garden with shrubs, trees, summerhouses, rockeries, fish ponds, splashing fountains, and space for all the flowers she could grow.

Shotbolt found time away from his business to be a good, public-spirited citizen. In the 1890s he was a pioneer subscriber to the B.C. Telephone Company. He was also one of the men of vision who organized the first electric light and street railway companies. At that time Fairfield Road ended at Foul Bay Road, just

warehouse at the rear. At the back was a laboratory, and on the second floor a five-room suite housed Shotbolt's growing family of three sons and a daughter.

In 1891 Shotbolt was first president of the B.C. Pharmaceutical Association, and by the turn of the century his store was entering its fifth successful decade. Choice perfumeries and toiletries filled the shelves. The pharmacy filled prescriptions for all the city's physicians with high-quality English, French, and American drugs. Shotbolt's own proprietary remedies were being shipped to all parts of the province. In the 1940s

outside the gates of "Hollywood." Although the Number 6 streetcar turned around there, Shotbolt didn't patronize it. Instead he drove himself into town—a journey of just under an hour in those days—or had his wife drive him. She would visit or go shopping and pick him up again at the end of the day.

Shotbolt was actively involved in the store until the day he died, in March 1922, at the age of 79. He was buried at Ross Bay Cemetery. Lavinia stayed in the house until her own death in 1945, at the age of 92. By 1950 the house and grounds, now neglected, had disappeared. A new subdivision sprang up in their place. The original driveway into the estate, now called Shotbolt Road, is the only reminder of the man who produced pills and potions for Victoria's pioneers.

In the 1890s, "Hollywood" still stood in solitary splendour at the base of Gonzales Hill. The Number 6 streetcar turned around at the gates, but Shotbolt preferred to drive. The journey from here to his downtown store took close to an hour.

Although he didn't use it himself, Thomas Shotbolt was involved in bringing the first streetcar service to Victoria. Here, one of the first cars makes its inaugural run in February 1890.

DINGLEY DELL

Fine home for the Fawcetts

The streetcar system that Thomas Shotbolt helped organize was a godsend. It afforded easier access to what had once been the outskirts of town. One area that became more popular was the south side of the Gorge, where the Fawcetts lived. But our story about the Fawcetts begins many years earlier, many miles away.

Edgar Fawcett was born in 1847 in Australia to Thomas and Jane Fawcett, formerly of Kidderminster, England. The Fawcetts had emigrated in 1838, intent on starting a business in Sydney, where Edgar, his brother Rowland, and sister Amy were born. In 1849 the family moved to San Francisco. After some years there, Thomas decided to take his family home.

He bought a ship, sent it up the West Coast for a load of lumber, and waited for it to return to California so the family could join it and sail to England. But the ship was wrecked in Barkley Sound. There was no insurance, and Thomas was ruined. A move back to Britain was out of the question; it would have to be somewhere closer to home. In 1858 he joined the throngs of gold miners migrating to B.C. and settled in Victoria. His family joined him the next year.

After an eleven-day voyage from San Francisco, Mrs. Fawcett, Edgar, and Rowland (Amy had died) sailed with 600 others into Esquimalt aboard the *Northerner*. Fifty years later, when Edgar published a book of his reminiscences, his first impressions of Victoria were still crystal clear. It was February 12, 1859.

> The first thing that attracted our attention on coming into the harbour was the high palisade of the fort ... The fort bell rang at six o'clock in the morning, when the gates at the east and west ends were opened, and at six o'clock in the evening they were closed. There were two large general stores, and many storehouses and barns inside, and at the stores you could buy anything from a needle to an anchor, from a gallon of molasses to the silk for a dress.
>
> Fort Street looked very different to what it does now [written in the early 1900s]. The roadbed was composed of boulders which, being round, made rough riding, and so muddy too! Try and imagine it. The sidewalk was of two-inch boards, laid lengthwise, three boards wide, I think, and commenced at the Brown Jug corner, running up for three or four blocks.
>
> Outside Johnson Street on the north, Blanchard [sic] Street on the east, and the north end of the James Bay bridge on the south, everything else was country—oak and pine trees, with paths only, otherwise trails made by Indians and cattle. Within this wood under the oaks were wildflowers of all kinds in profusion.

Myra and Edgar Fawcett

crisp, sweet apples were frequently "liberated" by the Fawcett boys. ("Many an apple have I had from this orchard," Fawcett wrote, "and apples were apples in those days, whatever they may be now.") Good duck shooting could be had at the lake on View Street east of Quadra.

A bridge across the harbour afforded access to the Songhees reserve, Esquimalt, and beyond. Outside the boundaries of Johnson Street and Blanshard Street, and along the south shore of James Bay, there was only forest and farmland.

Edgar and his brother followed a trail through the forest to the squared-log Colonial School at Yates and Ormond, where education could be had for a fee of five dollars per child, payable yearly in advance. They were joined in class by James, son of Governor Douglas, and the sons of Dr. W.F. Tolmie, former chief factor Roderick Finlayson, and Hillside Farm owner John Work. The Fawcetts bought their vegetables from Hillside Farm, which stretched from the Gorge to Cook Street and from Finlayson to Kings. Fawcett remembered:

> It took us the best part of a day to go to Hillside Farm for a sack of assorted vegetables. Several boys would start together for this trip into the country ... We started after breakfast and took our lunch, going across country by trail, each with a sack, which was filled by old Willie Pottinger, the gardener, for a shilling ... With our loads we started for home, and the further we got from Hillside the heavier the vegetables got, and therefore the more stoppages we made to rest. At last Fort and Blanchard Streets were in sight, and we were home again, tired out and hungry as hunters.

Once settled in a house on Kane (now Broughton) Street, the family had time to explore. There were only two brick buildings on Government Street—Thomas Harris's fine home and George Richardson's Victoria (later Windsor) Hotel. The deep ravine running between Johnson and Pandora streets into the harbour was bridged at Store, Government, and Douglas streets. Douglas and Johnson streets were lined with gold miners' tents.

The Hudson's Bay Company bakery was on Fort Street, which was bereft of buildings east of Douglas save for some HBC barns. Between Fort and Kane streets was a huge orchard, whose

Edgar, who would later attend the Collegiate School on Church Hill (now Burdett Avenue), was in turn a choirboy and organist at Christ Church.

The devout Fawcett was both choirboy and organist at Christ Church, on Church Hill.
Years after Fawcett's death, the Christ Church choir was led by choirmaster Herbert Kent.

An amusing incident occurred one Sunday evening when I, forgetting the number of verses of a hymn to be sung, stopped playing, and the congregation commenced another verse. Seeing that I had made an error I began again two notes behind. This made confusion worse confounded, as may be supposed, but having commenced I continued to the end of the verse. This being the closing hymn, "Lord, Dismiss Us With Thy Blessing," I was not long in making my exit from the church, as I did not wish to meet Mr. Cridge or any of the church officers.

He was also involved in more serious misdoing. Along with several other boys, he was, as he put it, "accidentally on purpose" responsible for a devastating fire at a Native burial site on Deadman's (now Halkett) Island.

The island, in Selkirk Water, contained shallow graves surrounded by picket fences and was covered with trees that supported wooden boxes containing the remains of the dead. The boys lit a fire, as was their custom. Then, curious to see if the boxes would burn, they piled pieces of wood under them and lit a match. Within minutes the flames spread and consumed all within their reach.

The paper next morning was early sought for, and with fear and trembling, too. There was good reason for fear, for the paper gave an account of the affair. The Indians had made complaint to the police, and they were searching for the culprits. I was afraid to go out at all, much less to go to school, and every knock at

Edgar Fawcett and his family stand outside "Dingley Dell." Their home, named after a house in a Charles Dickens novel, was the scene of many a fine Queen's Birthday gathering, when guests would sip tea under the large trees while watching the regatta on the Gorge.

In 1898, miners lined up outside the Customs House, where Fawcett worked as a clerk, to buy licences to dig for gold in the Klondike.

the door made me start. I at last confessed to my parents my share in the business ... lucky it was for me that I didn't get what I deserved, a good whipping, as my mother said.

Today, the bare rock face of Halkett Island, devoid of any evidence of trees, boxes, or bones, bears mute testament to the game that went horribly wrong.

Two more sons were born to the Fawcetts. Then when Edgar was fifteen, his mother died after a long and painful illness. She was laid to rest in the Quadra Street Burying Ground, a place that had always held a great fascination for him. He had wandered amongst the markers and marvelled at the variety of names recorded there. He had noted naval funerals, when gun carriages became mired in the mud on the Quadra Street Hill, and where one member of the burial party stood on the coffin while another member shovelled dirt on top to anchor it to its waterlogged grave.

By 1863 the local population had doubled. There were more churches, more banks, more saloons, and—at long last—a real theatre where Edgar and other members of the Victoria Amateur Dramatic Club could raise money for charity. Water flowed from Spring Ridge through wooden pipes. One dollar bought 40 buckets. Victoria now boasted a gasworks, and there were plans for a railway to connect the city with Esquimalt. Newly arrived immigrants settled on fertile farmland beyond the city limits. Soon it would no longer be necessary to import produce from foreign parts.

When Edgar left school he went into business with his brother as an upholsterer. He was among the first to join the Victoria Rifle Volunteers, paying 50 cents a month for dues, $26 for a uniform, and as much money as was needed for ammunition for target practice.

He remained active in the church and supported Reverend Edward Cridge's move to establish the Reformed Episcopal Church in 1876. That same year he married Myra Holden, who was eleven years his junior. They had three sons and three daughters and lived on Franklin (later Collinson) Street. Edgar changed careers, entering the dominion civil service in 1882 to become a clerk at the Customs House. In 1890 he moved his growing family to "Dingley Dell," a large house set in two acres on the south side of the Gorge. In all his writing, Edgar never explained why he gave the house this name, but he loved the novels of Charles Dickens, and "Dingley Dell" was Mr. Wardle's home in Dickens's *Pickwick Papers*.

Edgar retired in 1910, after 29 years as assistant appraiser in charge of the Postal Package and Express Office, and started studying local history. He died in 1923 at the age of 76 and was buried at Ross Bay. Myra lived on at "Dingley Dell" until her death at age 75 in 1933. The house was demolished some years later.

All that remains of the family now is a short street and an apartment building named after their home. But Edgar Fawcett's legacy lives on in *Some Reminiscences of Old Victoria*, a lively literary dip into the delights and disasters of pioneer life.

DAVIE STREET

Family of physicians and fearless leaders

When throat problems plagued fifteen-year-old Edgar Fawcett, he was treated by the father of a fellow choirboy. Forty years later, when typhoid struck, the former choirboy's brother would care for him. One way or another, the Davie family figured largely in Fawcett's—and British Columbia's—future.

John Chapman Davie Sr. spent his childhood in Devon, England, and left a medical practice in Surrey to bring his family to Vancouver Island in 1862. His wife, who was in poor health, stayed in England with her daughter and youngest son. Four other sons sailed around the Horn with their father on the *Anna Maria*. After his wife died in 1866, Dr. Davie, who was enamoured with the new city of Victoria, sent for the children he had left behind.

Setting up office at the corner of Government and Bastion, the doctor became a

While John Davie Jr. followed his father (centre) into the practice of medicine, Alexander (right) and Theodore Davie (left) studied law. Alexander sang alongside Edgar Fawcett in the Christ Church choir.

Dr. John Davie Jr. and his two wives, Kate (left) and Sara.

popular figure in town, always ready with a smile and a warm handshake as he steered his horse and buggy along the muddy streets. Two or three times a month he ventured on horseback to the Cowichan Valley, following trails formed by animals and used by the Natives. The journey was fraught with danger. "Take an axe with you," he warned other travellers in a letter to the *Colonist*. "My horse nearly smothered in a slough."

Sure that fresh air and country life would be healthier for his two middle sons, Horace and William, he bought 200 acres of land for each of them. They walked 60 miles through the forest to Somenos and developed farms there. Travellers on the long route north would soon be grateful; Horace ran the only blacksmith's shop between Victoria and Nanaimo.

Meanwhile, the Victoria-based Davies continued to entrench themselves in the daily doings of the rapidly growing city. Dr. Davie took an interest in politics and progress and became a member of the legislative council of the colony of British Columbia. Son Alexander, who sang in the Christ Church choir with Edgar Fawcett, studied law, as did his brother Theodore. John Chapman Davie Jr. attended medical school in San Francisco. He returned to Victoria after graduating in 1867, at the age of 21, and joined his father's practice.

In 1869 there was both sorrow and joy. Dr. John Davie Sr. died and was buried at St. Peter's, Quamichan. Dr. John Davie Jr. married Kate Thain. He moved his office first to Langley Street, then set up a home on Douglas Street. Three daughters were born in that house, where frantic nighttime knocks on the door would often send the doctor bumping off along rough country roads with his horse and buggy to see to a sick patient.

Dr. John Davie Jr. worked at both St. Joseph's Hospital (top) and the Royal (later Royal Jubilee) Hospital (below). Richard Maynard took this 1880s photograph of the Royal Jubilee's fine buildings surrounded by spacious grounds—the medical community's pride and joy.

By 1893, when the old Birdcages on the south side of the harbour were moved to make way for a brand-new legislative building, Attorney General Alexander Davie was dead. His brother Theodore was premier of B.C., and Dr. John Davie Jr. was about to become a widower for the second time.

Suddenly, in 1881, Kate died. She was only 29. Three years later the widower was married again, this time to Sara, eldest daughter of J.H. Todd. The Todds and the Davies had arrived in Victoria the same year and knew each other well. In Dr. Davie's case, perhaps too well. He had made Sara's acquaintance in Duncan while he was still married to Kate; indeed, it was said by some that poor Kate had died of a broken heart.

Sensing that Sara's father, who had been dismayed by the affair, would not approve of the marriage, the two arranged it without him. Father and daughter never repaired their relationship. The Davies, however, went from strength to strength. It was by all accounts a happy union. Sara adored her husband and was a loving stepmother to his three children. Dr. Davie built them a fine home on Rockland hill, where Sara entertained and became a respected member of Victoria society—everything, in fact, that her father had hoped she would be.

The good doctor's brothers were also respected members of B.C. society. When British Columbia premier William Smithe died suddenly in 1887, Attorney General Alexander Davie took his place. Davie tried to continue his law practice along with the premiership but succeeded only in exhausting himself. By August 1889 he was gone. His duties were taken over by John Robson, who died in London while on government business in 1892. The new premier was Robson's attorney general, Theodore Davie. In the six years before he too died, Davie was responsible for cementing Victoria's place as the capital of B.C.

While his brothers were embroiled in politics, Dr. Davie concentrated on public health. Sporadic outbreaks of smallpox had continued through the years, and in 1892 the *Colonist* applauded the doctor's appointment as provincial health officer. The government, said the *Colonist*, was alive to the dangers of the pestilence in other countries and determined that it should not gain a foothold in this fair land.

Dr. Davie was the first doctor at St. Joseph's Hospital and one of the first at the Royal Hospital, situated high on the Pandora Street rock. He was a skilful surgeon, always up to date on the latest techniques. In later years he was heavily involved in the design and planning of the Royal Jubilee Hospital, which opened in 1890 and was among the first in western Canada to adopt the antiseptic system discovered by Pasteur and perfected by Lister.

These activities helped keep his mind off thoughts of home. In 1894 disaster had struck again. Sara died of pneumonia at the age of 39, despite her husband's desperate attempts to save her. She was buried, somewhat ironically, at Ross Bay Cemetery beside first wife Kate.

Despite the fact that tuberculosis had left him with only one lung, Davie worked on, caring for his patients and never refusing to treat those who couldn't pay. In 1903 it was his insistence that Edgar Fawcett should rest after a bout of typhoid that spurred Fawcett to pen his reminiscences, which describe so many details of those early days.

Dr. Davie continued to be a ladies' man, but remained faithful to Sara by never marrying again. In 1911 he died and was buried at Quamichan beside his father. Davie Street, which doglegs from Brighton to Fort, remembers the men who, by one means or another, helped make Victoria what it is today.

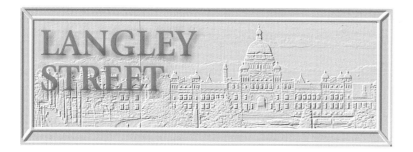

LANGLEY STREET

Brothers open first wholesale drugstore

Every doctor needs a good druggist, and the Davies were fortunate—Langley and Co. was but a few blocks north of Dr. John Davie Sr.'s office at Government and Broughton. A few years later, Dr. Davie Jr. opened his own office on Langley Street itself.

Alfred, James, and Charles Langley were born in Staffordshire, England. In 1849 they followed the world to California in search of gold. Unlike most adventurers, they were unprepared for gold fever, but—being two chemists and an accountant—they were well equipped to treat fevers of another kind.

By the time the gold rush slowed to a ramble, the two eldest Langley brothers were ready to move on. Leaving Charles in San Francisco, Alfred and James travelled north with the new wave of gold seekers and wasted no time in opening the first wholesale and retail drugstore in the rapidly growing town of Victoria. The Langley brothers opened for business July 14, 1858, on the south side of Yates Street, near Wharf. At this time, Yates was a wide dirt street lined with wooden buildings and planked sidewalks. It was also one of the busiest streets in town, its hastily erected hotels and saloons making life more comfortable for hundreds of mostly temporary residents.

With the offices of Drs. Helmcken and Davie close by, the Langleys did a roaring trade. Like most businesses of its time, Apothecaries Hall was more than just a drugstore. As well as imported drugs, chemicals, and patent medicines, the establishment advertised perfumery, fancy goods, paints and paintbrushes, coal oil lamps, window glass, and varnishes. But it was as druggists that the brothers became best known.

Alfred and Mary Langley

Alfred was appointed a provisional member of the legislative council of British Columbia in 1861. A year later he returned to England to attend the International Exhibition in

*Alfred and Mary pose with
four of their five children.*

justice of the peace and was appointed to the board of education. He and Mary lived for a time on the south side of Fort Street, in a house that stands to this day, but later moved to "The Maples," perched high on the rock at Fairfield Road and Moss Street. The house sat in a terraced garden with rockeries and pools that looked south and west over Beacon Hill Park and the Sooke Hills. In 1876 Mary died after a brief illness at the age of 37. Her widower didn't marry again.

James, meanwhile, had married Anna Maria Thain in 1861. Annie, as she was called, had arrived in Victoria from New Brunswick with her parents in 1852. James and Annie had three sons and by 1892 were living at "Fairview," a stone-and-iron-fenced mansion on the corner of Quebec and Menzies streets. Immediately to the east were the sweeping lawns of the government buildings, known as "The Birdcages," and the wooden James Bay Bridge. Beyond and to the south, the fine homes of James Bay were reminders that the area had been Victoria's first and finest residential community before the rich and famous removed to the Rockland area.

London's Hyde Park. While there he married an Irish girl by the name of Mary and brought her back to Victoria. They would have five children together.

As a druggist, Alfred Langley felt some responsibility for the good health of Victorians. He was concerned by the outbreaks of deadly diseases that often swept the town and in 1868 asked the editor of the *Colonist* to print what he described as "an almost infallible" remedy for diphtheria. It was a solution of potassium chlorate, hydrochloric acid, and water, to be used to "gargle wash the throat frequently. A portion will necessarily be swallowed, which," he maintained, "will do no injury."

By 1872 Alfred had become more involved in government and community affairs. He was a

James and Annie Langley

When Alfred Langley was in England in 1862, he attended the International Exhibition in London's Hyde Park, where early Victoria resident Sarah Crease's sketches of the colony of Vancouver Island were being viewed with great interest. This drawing shows a view of the Gorge waterway.

The Langley brothers retained control of their store until 1885, when they took in a partner from Montreal, and in 1894 James Langley resigned active management of the firm to the Henderson brothers. James died at the age of 70 in November 1895, just five months before Alfred, who died at "The Maples" in April 1896, aged 75. The estate was sold out to the Hendersons, who closed the retail drug department and moved the headquarters of the company to Vancouver.

The sole survivor of the original foursome, Annie lived on at "Fairview." By the time she died there at the age of 74, in 1912, the Birdcages were gone. In their place, fulfilling the vision of Premier Theodore Davie, imposing new Parliament Buildings loomed large over the Inner Harbour. Passenger ships docked on Belleville Street, a fine new hotel on the harbour's east side—the Empress—catered to an ever-increasing number of visitors, and in the heart of downtown, Langley Street connected Yates and Broughton streets, running along the east side of the block where two brothers made their mark as pioneer druggists in this town.

From coalmaster's wife to castle dweller

*A*nnie Langley probably knew little about the two women who had once presided over her James Bay home. They represented two generations of one famous family. Laura, wife of James Dunsmuir, had been the most recent occupant at "Fairview." Before that, the matriarch of the mansion was James's mother, Joan. Mrs. Dunsmuir Sr. had come a long way from her humble beginnings in Ayrshire, Scotland, to the city of Victoria—and the most incredible episode of her life story was still to be penned.

Joan and Robert Dunsmuir

Johanna, known as Joan, White married Robert Dunsmuir in 1847. In 1850, Robert's uncle persuaded him to sign a contract with the Hudson's Bay Company to work at a coal mine on the northeast coast of Vancouver Island. Joan, by this time the mother of two infant daughters and pregnant with another child, found herself on board the HBC ship *Pekin*, which sailed around Cape Horn and arrived at Fort Vancouver, in the Oregon Territory, just in time for Joan to give birth to her first son, James.

The Dunsmuirs sailed on up the coast of Vancouver's Island to Fort Rupert, close to where Port McNeill is today. Living conditions were primitive, to say the least. The Dunsmuirs' "regulation" two-room log cabin had a bare, earthen floor spread with crushed clamshells. A pot-bellied stove sat in the centre. A few metres away, the fort's large bake oven served as the main cooking facility for all the people employed there.

A few years later the mining at Fort Rupert came to an end. Colonial surveyor J.D. Pemberton had confirmed the existence of coal mines at Nanaimo, so Robert and his family moved there, along with the rest. But when he was offered another contract in 1854, Robert declined. He was willing to stay in Nanaimo, he said, but as an independent businessman. He would develop and manage coal seams and sell the coal to the HBC.

The Dunsmuirs' house at Wellington was a far cry from the simple log cabin they had moved into more than twenty years earlier. Robert was now one of the wealthiest men in Nanaimo. He and Joan were the parents of two boys and eight girls.

After several false starts he struck a seam that was to make him as rich as the coal it contained. In 1869, with fifteen years' mine management experience under his belt, he was looking for investors. Royal Navy officers in the area were looking to invest. It was the perfect combination. Several naval men helped Dunsmuir parlay his Wellington Colliery into a small fortune as he supplied the booming population of San Francisco with Vancouver Island coal.

Fourteen years later, when the original investors had sold their interest back to him, Wellington was worth more than $1 million.

Some said Robert had made his fortune on the backs of his miners—he paid them poorly, and there were rumours that men's lives were sacrificed to unsafe conditions in the mines.

Robert paid them no heed. Already wealthy beyond his wildest dreams, he signed a contract to build the newly proposed Island rail line linking Nanaimo and Esquimalt, becoming the richest man on Vancouver Island. The contract fit his plans perfectly. Over the years, Joan had produced another son and several more daughters, and he had built a series of homes to house the growing family. The sons had joined the family firm, but by 1882 only three of the

Perched on the top of the Fort Street hill, Dunsmuir's incredible Craigdarroch Castle (pictured from the Fort Street entrance) was a sight to behold. He could not have dreamed that, long after his demise, his castle would still be the focus of attention for admiring visitors.

girls had married; that left five for whom suitable husbands still had to be found.

Acknowledging his own political aspirations and his desire to see his daughters marry well, Robert decided to follow the rail line south. The Victoria of the early 1880s bore no comparison to the HBC outpost of days gone by. The fort was long gone. The Douglas days were over, although Lady Amelia, Sir James's widow, was still active on the social scene. And it was this social scene that interested the senior Dunsmuirs the most.

The city was full of Navy types—good marriage material—and there was fine land to be had near the governor's residence. Robert bought a five-and-a-half-acre parcel—the first of a series of purchases that eventually netted him more than 28 acres of prime Victoria real estate. Inspired by the grand San Francisco homes of his California business associates,

Two years after Robert Dunsmuir died, sixth daughter Jessie married Sir Richard Musgrave in an elaborate ceremony that included no fewer than 27 young female attendants.

Robert determined to build himself an equally impressive edifice, something in the Scottish baronial style, with towers and turrets and tall chimneys, perched on a hill with a 360-degree view. In short, a sort of a castle.

While his dream became reality, Robert moved his family into a temporary home in James Bay. The large dwelling at the corner of Quebec and Menzies streets belonged to an American captain whose move away from Victoria had coincided conveniently with the Dunsmuirs' arrival. Mother, father, and five daughters moved in. James was still in Nanaimo, taking care of business at the colliery. Alexander was running the San Francisco office.

Work on the castle began in 1888. Robert and Joan named it "Craigdarroch," after a tiny hamlet in Dumfriesshire. It cost more than half a million dollars to build—a massive sum in those days. Supplies and materials came from Scotland, England, Italy, and the eastern U.S. Rugs were bought from India and Persia, and pictures from the art galleries of Europe.

Still living at "Fairview," Joan enjoyed an opulent lifestyle, ordering gowns from Paris and hats from New York. One by one her daughters were paraded before the cream of Victoria society, which was amused by, if not entirely accepting of, the new, not always terribly ladylike arrivals. "Craigdarroch" was only a year away from completion. The stage was set for a fabulous future.

But then the unthinkable happened. Robert took to his bed with what seemed like a severe cold. Less than a week later, he was dead at 64.

His grieving widow took her two youngest unmarried daughters on a protracted trip to Europe. James, now 38, and Alexander, 36, were left to oversee completion of the sandstone and brick monument to their father's wealth. In May 1890 Alex went to England to bring his mother home to "Craigdarroch," or Dunsmuir Castle as it was known. James, newly arrived from Nanaimo, moved his family into the now-vacant "Fairview." By that time, both brothers had faced the unbelievable truth: the father they had worked for all their lives, believing they would inherit his fortune, had betrayed them. His will, shocking in its simplicity, was one page long. It left his entire estate—coal mines, carriers, shares, railroad interests, and the castle—to Joan.

Thus began one of the most bitter, bizarre legal battles in Victoria's history, and the beginning of another Dunsmuir era—one that would end in 1908 with Joan's death as a near recluse in the castle she called home.

BURLEITH CRESCENT

Grand house on the Gorge for Dunsmuir's son

The contents of Robert Dunsmuir's Last Will and Testament sent shock waves rippling through his family. Even if she had displayed sound business sense, in 1880s Victoria it was considered outrageous for a man to publicly acknowledge a woman's fitness to carry on his affairs. But Robert's instructions were clear. His sons had invested their energies in his empire, but he didn't consider them capable of controlling it. He left that job to his wife Joan.

Joan Dunsmuir was now over 60. It was almost 40 years since she and Robert had arrived in Fort Rupert with their infant son. It was said that the blond, blue-eyed toddler was so admired by local Native women that they had even tried to buy him from his mother. When she refused, they "borrowed" him, taking him from his cradle one day when Joan was cooking food for her family at the fort.

Lieutenant-Governor James Dunsmuir

Joan organized a search party, which found a group of Kwakiutl women clustered around a fire, passing the bundle that was baby James reverently from hand to hand. They wanted him for their next chief, they said. Joan told them he was to be chief of his own people, and took him home. In those days it seemed he was destined for great things; yet here he was, 38 years old and still not master of his own fate.

Both boys had contributed a great deal to their father's success. James, who had studied mine engineering south of the border, was solid and dependable. He and his American wife, Laura, raised a total of ten children, and James strove diligently to be what his father wanted him to be—a reliable, hard-working plodder.

Alex was the sparky one—bright and quick and energetic. Robert sent him to San Francisco to run the office there. He threw himself into the task and succeeded as a businessman. Unfortunately he fell foul of his parents on the personal level. He became enamoured of a married woman by the name of Josephine. She divorced her husband and moved in with Alex, but Robert and Joan refused to acknowledge her and warned their son that "that woman from San Francisco" would never be welcome in their home.

In 1892, two years after moving into "Fairview," James had the Queen Anne-style "Burleith" built for his family on the south side of the Gorge, an area that rivalled Rockland as the most desirable residential area. James's estate occupied twenty acres of land between present-day Burleith Crescent and Sunnyside Avenue, with tennis courts, croquet lawns, bridle paths, and a front-row view of summer activities and regattas on the Gorge waterway. Alexander remained in San Francisco with Josephine.

On the surface, not much had changed. Before, they had laboured for their father; now their mother held the reins. Then came the most galling part of all. The two men watched helplessly as their mother started to fritter away the Dunsmuir fortune on marriages and mansions for the girls.

In an attempt to balance the scales, James and Alex fought to gain control over at least part of the family business. Seven long years later they managed to get Joan to agree to make the San Francisco office a joint stock company, with shares divided equally between them, on condition that each brother's shares reverted to her should they die.

They tried to capitalize on their success by offering to buy Wellington Collieries from Joan, with payments to be made over ten years and interest to be paid to her on the outstanding balance. Their sisters complained bitterly that

Laura Dunsmuir with her youngest daughter, Dola.

James and Laura Dunsmuir's huge home on the Gorge was surrounded by beautifully landscaped gardens that featured croquet lawns, tennis courts, and a fabulous waterfront playground for the children. Parts of "Burleith's" stone wall can still be seen today along the north side of Craigflower Road.

the two men were taking advantage of their mother, but eventually Joan agreed to sign.

Alex was overjoyed. At last he was a man of independent means and could marry the woman who had waited patiently for almost twenty years. But tragedy was waiting in the wings. The two were still honeymooning in New York when Alex collapsed and died. Decades of high living had caught up with him at last. He lost his life to acute alcohol poisoning at the age of 46.

Then came another shock. When Alexander's will was read, it became clear that he had reneged on the agreement with his mother. He didn't leave his company shares to Joan. He left them to the premier of British Columbia—his brother James.

The sisters, incensed, persuaded their mother that James had turned Alex against all of them. They were surprised to discover a potential ally in their new sister-in-law, who was now reliant on James for her share of income from Alex's estate. Josephine and James came to an agreement, but when Josephine died in 1902 of breast cancer, opposition to Alex's will came from another unexpected quarter—Edna, Josephine's daughter by her first husband.

Edna accused James of exerting undue influence on her mother to hand over her claim to Alexander's fortune. Joan hesitated to support anyone remotely related to a woman whose existence she had always denied, but eventually she waded into the fray. Victorians twittered in

*In 1901, James and Laura posed with their children on the day
daughter Sarah Byrd married Major Guy Mortimer Audain.*

After building a castle to rival "Craigdarroch" on a 650-acre estate in Colwood, James and Laura enjoyed taking tea with their family on the patio overlooking Esquimalt Lagoon.

amazement. In 1906 the case was settled ... in favour of James. He had won, but at tremendous cost. His mother refused to see or speak to him again, even when her health was failing and he, as lieutenant governor, was living in Government House, practically at the bottom of her garden.

When James's term at Government House came to an end, he did not go back to "Burleith." He wanted to build a castle, as his father had done, and he commissioned an architect to design one, based on an Elizabethan manor house in Warwickshire. "Hatley Castle" was three times larger than "Craigdarroch" and contained 22 bedrooms and 9 bathrooms. It was situated in Hatley Park, a 650-acre estate in Colwood. On the grounds there was an Italian garden, a Japanese garden, and housing for more than 100 maintenance workers.

When Joan died, "Craigdarroch"—left to her five daughters but too expensive for any one of them to maintain—was disposed of, the contents sold at public auction, the land subdivided, and the castle thrown in as a draw prize for one of the

Dominating their Hatley Park estate, James and Laura's exquisite home served as a centre for Victoria's social elite. Today the estate houses Royal Roads University.

lot purchasers. It ended up the property of a couple called Cameron. They lost it in the pre-World War I economic downslide. It became a convalescent home, then headquarters of the Victoria School Board, and finally site of the Victoria School of Music before it was restored as a heritage site in the early 1960s.

James died in 1920 and left everything to Laura and their nine surviving children. In 1927 Laura died, and again, no single one of the children could afford to run their castle. A couple of years later, Hatley Park was purchased for a song by the federal government, and in 1941 it became HMCS Royal Roads, a training facility for navy and air force personnel. Later it became Royal Roads Military College and is now a private university. Like "Craigdarroch," "Hatley Castle" is a reminder of a family whose fortune brought only bitterness and disappointment.

WEILER AVENUE

Furniture supplier for fine homes and castles

*A*t the opposite end of Fort Street from Craigdarroch, another pioneer was making a name for himself. John Weiler was the first in his family to supply furnishings for Victoria's finer homes and castles.

Weiler was born in Germany in 1824. Like many others, he came to Victoria via California, enticed there at the age of 26 by the gold rush and the prospect of making money as a miner and stock rancher. In 1855 he married Christiana Kessel, also a native of Germany, who had travelled across America with her parents some years before.

John and Christiana Weiler

By the early 1860s the family included four children, and Weiler was ready to try his luck in the gold fields farther north. The family set out for the Cariboo but was sidetracked by the promise of even better pickings in Victoria. The Weilers found themselves in a newly incorporated city that was proud of its beginnings but eager to move beyond them. With the influx of Cariboo-bound gold miners, the tiny Hudson's Bay Company settlement had taken on a life of its own. In place of the HBC, independent businesses served the growing community. Spreading out like fingers from the city's core, Victoria's streets pointed the way to the future. Families built homes along them. And homes had to be furnished.

Weiler started small. Working for others until he was established, he went into partnership in 1862 and opened a modest upholstery and furniture store on Government Street. Stemler & Weiler became Weiler's own a few years later when he bought out his partner and moved the business to Fort Street, between Broad and Douglas.

By the end of the 1870s he was firmly ensconced at the corner of Fort and Broad in a building erected by grocer and soon-to-be-mayor James Fell. In the 1882 City Directory,

In the 1880s, Weiler (right) was pictured with his sons outside John Weiler, Upholsterer and Paperhanger, at premises above James Fell's grocery store at Fort and Broad streets.

"John Weiler, Upholsterer & Paperhanger," advertised everything from oilcloth and carpets to cornices and window blinds, from mattresses and lounge sets to crockery and cutlery.

Sons George, Charles, Otto, and Joseph joined their father's business as soon as their schooling was finished. The five worked closely, with each son responsible for a specific business function. By the late 1880s the company's brick "warerooms" on the northeast corner of Broad and Broughton, erected in 1884, then enlarged to three times their original size, couldn't cope with the demand.

A four-storey extension was added to the small factory John Weiler had built on Humboldt Street, just east of the wooden James Bay Bridge. The company name, displayed in large white letters across the extension's front

and rear walls, could be seen from far and wide. Equipped with what a promotional booklet described as "the most modern improved machinery," the factory employed more than 60 men, whose fine woodwork and upholstered furniture graced local offices, commercial establishments, and family homes.

For some years John and Christiana Weiler had been living at Blanshard and Broughton, close to the factory and the store, but far enough away from the commercial centre to enjoy pleasant summer evenings on the porch or in the garden. In 1891 John Weiler handed over the business to his sons and contemplated a leisurely retirement.

With the four as equal partners, Weiler Brothers went from strength to strength. Their

In the late 1890s, the four-storey addition to Weiler's original factory, shown here in a view west down Church Hill (now Burdett Avenue) toward a distant Laurel Point, was the largest building on the Humboldt Street waterfront.

huge showroom on the southeast corner of Government and Broughton carried every conceivable household item. The "Furniture, Carpets, Wallpaper and Complete House Furnishings" advertised in big white letters on the building's side wall were carefully chosen and tastefully displayed. Imported glassware and silverware gleamed in the light from huge arched windows. An elevator whisked shoppers from floor to floor. You could order your piece of furniture at Government and Broughton, then go round the corner to the factory to watch it being made.

The Weiler name was synonymous with quality. The brothers landed lucrative contracts.

Their clients included the most successful local companies like Pither & Leiser Ltd., liquor and tobacco merchants; the Temple Building at Blanshard and Pandora; wealthy Rockland residents; and the family whose fairytale castle stood atop Fort Street hill.

Otto was in charge of advertising. In 1881 he had amazed Victoria by producing a catalogue—the city's first—promoting Weiler wares. Thirty years later the Weiler catalogue had mushroomed to 350 pages of items, pictured and described in detail, along with enticements to visit the store, view the wares, and compare the value. An upholstered chesterfield sofa covered in chintz or taffeta could be had for

This view north from the recently completed Parliament Buildings shows the huge sign on the side of the Weiler showroom, which stands there to this day. At the turn of the century, water still filled the bay to the right of the bridge.

under $100. A chair covered in Spanish leather cost just $60. Oak and silver butter dishes were $2 each. As an added incentive, cash purchases earned a 10 percent discount, or "good terms" could be arranged.

By that time—1912—Otto's father and two of his brothers were gone. John Weiler had died in 1899, Joseph in 1901, and George seven years later. A sister, Emma, had married and moved to Seattle. Christiana, who moved in with son Charles after her husband's death, lived until 1917. She was 91 when she, too, was buried at Ross Bay.

In the summer of 1912, Otto and Charles cut off their active connection with the business and retired to enjoy the fruits of their labours. The firm continued under the family name until the early 1930s.

Today an avenue in Sidney reminds us of a hard-working family that made good in Victoria. Visitors to Craigdarroch Castle can view a chest of drawers bearing the company's brass nameplate, a tiny china teacup showing the castle's likeness, which was made for Weiler Brothers in Austria. And on the southeast corner of Government and Broughton, the Weiler Building stands as tall and as proud as when John Weiler built it, more than a century ago.

WILSPENCER PLACE

Minding the family store

The Weilers weren't the only ones looking after Victoria's home and business needs. Just a few blocks to the north, the Spencer family was also having an effect on the local retail scene.

Patriarch David Spencer was Welsh-born, a Glamorgan boy who apprenticed in dry goods after leaving school. He was in his early twenties when he sailed from Liverpool in 1862. Landing in New York, he made his way to Panama, crossed the isthmus, and continued up the West Coast by steamer.

He was too late to try for gold in the Cariboo, but in perfect time to serve those who had been successful there. In the newly incorporated city of Victoria, where grizzled gold miners mingled with society matrons and middle-class folks from the Old Country, Spencer found his niche. The city was like him—young and energetic. It had stores, saloons, and brothels galore, theatres,

David and Emma Spencer

newspapers, and much, much more. But there were few places in the midst of the hustle and bustle where someone could sit quietly and catch up with the news of the day.

By the fall of 1864, Spencer's bookstore and reading room was open for business. It wasn't the first to provide such a service and wouldn't be the last, but for now it was a way to make money. For a fee, someone entering the reading room could gain access to all the latest newspapers and books they could read. The monthly fee was one dollar—cheap at twice the price for people who were thirsty for news and knowledge of happenings back home.

Business was brisk. Before long, Spencer had expanded his business to include a stationery store. Some years later he sold that store and went into partnership with one William Denny. In 1873 they bought a dry-goods store at the

In 1873, David Spencer's first dry-goods store, called "Victoria House," stood at the corner of Fort and Douglas streets.

corner of Fort and Douglas streets, and for the next five years sold exclusive dry goods imported from England.

Within a decade Spencer had bought Denny out and continued the business on his own. By 1882 his store was fairly bulging at the seams. More property was purchased. Spencer's store now stretched across the middle of a city block, with frontage on two streets and an arcade connecting them. If you entered on Broad Street and kept walking, you could end up on Government Street without ever leaving Spencer property. Not many people owned such a huge chunk of one block, and their lots usually fronted onto one street or another.

Victorians were aghast. The store was too big for a small city, they thought. But Spencer proved himself to be a man of vision. The day of the department store was dawning. As time went by he bought more property, extending his store frontage behind huge plate-glass windows along Broad and Government streets. Kitchenware, appliances, furniture, china, clothes, and shoes now vied with dry goods for customers' attention. His store compared favourably, declared the *Colonist*, with leading stores of the entire Pacific coast including San Francisco. Expansion to other areas was a foregone conclusion.

At the end of each day, Spencer hurried home to his wife and the family that seemed to

By the end of the 1870s, Spencer had moved his large family to a grand new home called "The Poplars" at the southwest end of the James Bay Bridge, where the Royal B.C. Museum is today. The road leading south from the bridge beside the first Parliament Buildings, or Birdcages (at right), was called Birdcage Walk and was later a continuation of Government Street.

be growing as fast as his business. Emma Lazenby, a native of Yorkshire, England, had arrived in Victoria in 1863, a year after her future husband. She had taken a different route, sailing around Cape Horn on the same storm-tossed ship whose late arrival had caused cabinet-maker Charles Hayward such anguish as he waited for his beloved Sarah.

David Spencer and Emma were married in the Methodist Church at Broad and Pandora streets in 1867. Their first child, born within the year, was quickly followed by twelve more. In the mid-1870s Spencer moved his family to James Bay. Within a few years of their arrival on

Menzies Street, he had built a home, "The Poplars," at the south end of the James Bay Bridge, right opposite Weiler's furniture factory. The location, at the corner of Belleville and Birdcage Walk, was ideal. West of "The Poplars," across the grassy apron fronting the Parliament Buildings, was "Fairview," future home of the Langleys and the Dunsmuirs. North across the bridge, within walking distance, was the store. A few blocks south was the ocean—a healthier playground for the young Spencers than the smelly mudflats of James Bay.

The best thing about working at one end of the bridge and living at the other was that the

A dedicated churchgoer and choirmaster, David Spencer Sr. helped establish the James Bay Methodist (now United) Church, which stands to this day near the corner of Menzies and Michigan streets.

family had ample warning of Father's return. He was an easily recognizable figure, with his top hat and long, flowing beard, hair always immaculately brushed, and clothing appropriate to his station as a successful businessman. The children took it in turns to watch out for him, so that dinner could be served the minute he walked through the door.

David and Emma Spencer were devout Methodists and had been active at the Pandora Street church from earliest times. Welshmen will always find a way to have music in their lives, and Spencer was no exception. He started, and for many years conducted, the first church choir and was instrumental in establishing James Bay Methodist (now United) Church at Menzies and Michigan streets.

As the five Spencer sons followed their father into the family business, a second store opened in Nanaimo. "Mr. Chris" moved to Vancouver to open a third. Eventually there would be nine Spencer stores in B.C. and one in Alberta. Nothing, it seemed, could stop the Spencer roller coaster of success. In 1910, when a disastrous fire levelled the Victoria store, Spencer was quick to regroup. He bought a nearby hotel, filled it with stock from his Vancouver store, and was open again for business within three weeks.

Rallying quickly after the devastating October 1910 fire that destroyed his store, Spencer arranged temporary space for his operation in the Driard Hotel (shown in background) and erected a sign to tell his customers that it would soon be "business as usual." The second Spencer store, built on the same site, was destroyed by fire in 1922.

Chris Spencer

In 1906, a few years after the senior Spencers moved to "Llan Derwen" (now the Art Gallery of Greater Victoria on Moss Street), they hosted a Methodist Conference group there. The group is pictured in front of the beautiful old mansion, which at that time stood proud and alone on this section of the Fort Street hill.

Early in the 1900s the senior Spencers moved to a beautiful mansion on Moss Street called "Llan Derwen," which in Welsh means "under the oaks." David Spencer died there in 1920, at the age of 82. Emma died in 1934, at the age of 92.

After his father's death, "Mr. Will" managed the Victoria store. When he died in 1946, his sister, the redoubtable "Miss Sara," took over. "Mr. Chris" stayed in Vancouver, where in 1948 he witnessed the end of an era as David Spencer's Ltd. became the property of the T. Eaton Co.

The remarkable Spencer family is remembered at the Art Gallery, the former Moss Street family home, which was donated to the city by "Mr. Chris" and "Miss Sara"; at David Spencer Jr.'s "Spencer Castle" on Cook Street; and in a street in the Rockland area named after "Mr. Will."

Publican pioneered in brick

*I*f David Spencer had been a drinking man, he might have been tempted by a trip to the bar at the end of a busy day. He didn't even have to cross the street. Two blocks closer to James Bay, on the same side of Government Street as his store, was George Richardson's Windsor Hotel.

The English-born Richardson was just 23 years old when he boarded the *Norman Morison* at Gravesend in October 1849. He was in good company. More than 80 souls were aboard, most journeying to Vancouver Island as contracted employees of the Hudson's Bay Company. Many of them, such as Field, Gillespie,

George and Mary Ann Richardson

Horne, Mills, Wain, and Whiffen, would later be remembered in city streets.

One of Richardson's seagoing companions eventually became a business neighbour—the ship's surgeon, Dr. J.S. Helmcken, later dispensed medical advice from his office a few blocks away

on Fort Street. But when the *Norman Morison* sailed into Esquimalt Harbour in the early spring of 1850, all that was yet to come.

No doubt the two men had quite different ideas about what life had in store for them as they trudged the muddy trail to the fort. Helmcken, who had dealt with smallpox and death on the long sea journey, doubtless envisaged a lifetime of service to sick people. Richardson espied a small settlement with potential that he fully intended to exploit. Five years later, with money in his pocket and 300 acres of land northeast of town, he was ready to sail back to England and find a bride.

Mary Ann Parker, eleven years George's junior, hailed from Kent. The newlyweds returned to Victoria on the *Princess Royal*, arriving in early 1858. Their timing was perfect. The first rush of Fraser River-bound gold miners arrived from San Francisco two

George Richardson erected the first brick hotel in Victoria in 1860, narrowly beating out a fellow hotelier for the honour. He originally called it the Victoria Hotel, later renamed it the Windsor Hotel, and in 1876 almost destroyed it completely in a freak accident. The building's fine arches are gone now and it houses retail stores, but it still stands at the northeast corner of Government and Courtney streets.

months later. Gearing up for gold digging was thirsty work. These men needed a drink. And George Richardson was ready and willing to serve them.

Before the gold rush slowed to a saunter, more than 20,000 hopefuls hauled their gear along Victoria's dusty roads. The 1860 City Directory lists saloons, restaurants, and a total of eight hotels in the downtown core. These were mostly wooden buildings, hastily erected to cater to the newcomers' needs. But Richardson catered to the more discriminating

miner. His Victoria Hotel, on the east side of Government at Rae (now Courtney), was built of brick.

By 1864 the city was in a post-gold rush slump. Richardson, tired of downtown living, leased his hotel to another man and moved his growing family out to his farm on North Park. But in the mid-1870s he was back in business, running the hotel himself. And in the fall of 1876 he was the victim of a most unfortunate accident, which the *Colonist* reported in detail the following day.

*George and Mary Ann Richardson's son and five daughters survived the 1876 blast.
All but one of the six were married by the time their mother died in 1911.
They buried their father beside her, at Ross Bay Cemetery, in 1922.*

The family had apparently retired to the hotel's upper level for the night when they suddenly became aware of a strong odour emanating from below. It was gas. Richardson lit a candle, followed his nose down to the front sitting room, and opened the door. The resulting explosion was heard half a mile away.

Inside the hotel, said the *Colonist*, the force of the blast blew down brick partitions, tore plaster from the walls, and wrenched doors from their frames. The parlour and dining room were wrecked. The stairs were partly destroyed. Ignited gas rushed up the stairwell and blew windows out on the upper level. Shattered glass littered the street below.

Miraculously, no one was seriously hurt. One can only imagine the horror Mary Ann must have felt, surrounded by terrified children and certain that her husband had been killed. But Richardson, who suffered severely singed hair and a burned hand, lived to tell the tale, and fortunately, reported the *Colonist*, the damage could be repaired.

In the late 1880s the Richardsons were living in a large home with porches and huge bay windows at 5 Gordon Street. The 1889 directory lists the Douglas House Hotel on the southwest corner of Douglas and Courtney under Mary Ann's name. By 1895, Richardson was listed as proprietor of both the Victoria House (formerly the Douglas House) and the Windsor Hotel (the old Victoria Hotel on Government at Rae).

In the early 1890s Richardson followed David Spencer and shipmate Dr. Helmcken

Twenty years after Richardson opened his hotel, anyone wandering along Government Street would tread a very different path to the one we follow today. Its surface was still rough—dusty in summer, a sea of mud in winter. Thoughtful storekeepers created covered walkways over raised plank sidewalks to protect customers from the elements.

across the James Bay Bridge. The Richardsons lived at the western end of Quebec Street for a while, then moved to 115 Government Street. From there it was only a short walk north to the Parliament Buildings and the Inner Harbour.

Mary Ann died at the Government Street house in 1911, aged 74. George lived another 11 years, dying in 1922 at the ripe old age of 96. Mourned by their surviving children—five

daughters and a son—they were buried side by side at Ross Bay Cemetery.

Fairfield's Richardson Street was probably named after a geological surveyor who sailed the B.C. coast in the 1870s. But along with Oak Bay's Windsor Road, it serves as a handy reminder of the man who was once the proud proprietor of Victoria's first brick hotel.

MUNRO STREET

From PSAC accountant to HBC chief factor

A few blocks from George Richardson's James Bay home, opposite the northwest corner of Beacon Hill Park, the Munro family entertained Victoria's high society.

Alexander Munro was born in Scotland in 1824. After leaving school he moved to London and was a bank clerk there for many years. At the age of 33 he accepted a position with the Puget's Sound Agricultural Company (PSAC), a Hudson's Bay Company subsidiary that had developed farms on the southern tip of Vancouver Island. Munro was to be PSAC's accountant and general overseer for the area.

Leaving his family to follow at a later date, Munro set sail for the New World. He arrived at Esquimalt, via Panama and San Francisco, in June 1857. At the end of that same year, Munro's wife Jane and their three daughters undertook an uncomfortable, storm-tossed voyage around Cape Horn on the *Princess Royal*. The family was reunited in early 1858.

By that time, the serene and peaceful settlement had turned into a way station for weary gold seekers. Exhausted after a rough voyage up the coast, but exhilarated by the thought of the riches that awaited them, hundreds of men camped out in tents near present-day Douglas and Johnson streets. Once supplies were purchased and passages booked, they journeyed on to the Fraser River, and other new arrivals took their place.

Before long the flow began to reverse. Men who had been successful—or unsuccessful—in the gold fields returned to Victoria, some to begin the long journey home, others to stay. Businessmen hurried to serve the growing population. The town became a city, with a mayor and council elected by the public and ready to make positive changes. Victoria's future seemed assured.

Alexander and Jane Munro

The large house at 645 Michigan Street, depicted in a sketch by daughter Jane, provided the perfect setting for the weddings of Alexander Munro's three daughters and many other friends. Today, the South Park School playing field covers the original site of the Munro home.

Meanwhile, across the harbour to the west, PSAC enterprises were not faring so well. Starting in 1850, PSAC had hired bailiffs to manage the four farms that covered most of Esquimalt. After seven years, the first bailiff, Donald Macaulay, had managed to develop only a small portion of his farm's 600 rocky, densely forested acres. For various reasons, his fellow farmers also fell short of expectations. Despite the company's best efforts, the venture was doomed to fail. Disappointed by the poor returns from the four farms, the HBC took over PSAC's assets in the mid-1860s.

Munro was now working for the HBC rather than PSAC. By this time he had built a large house for his growing family in James Bay, not far from the homes owned by Governor James Douglas and his daughter and son-in-law, Cecilia and Doctor J.S. Helmcken.

At that time, much of the central portion of James Bay—covered with pine trees and known as Beckley Farm—was still undeveloped. Along its northern perimeter, Governor Douglas's house stood close to the government buildings known as the Birdcages. Water lapped onto the beach just beyond a border of large

Looking across the north end of Beacon Hill Park, not far from the Munro residence, in the late 1880s. This view of Alderman (now Goodacre) Lake shows an island with an Indian tepee (left), and on the horizon above it, the original Christ Church Cathedral on Church Hill. Today, tall trees and banks of rhododendrons block the view to the north.

trees until Belleville Street replaced the trail established by the Native people that used to wind along the shoreline. James Bay Bridge, a fragile wooden structure that straddled the bay in a direct line south from Government Street, was more than adequate for the light carriages of the day.

Standing at the east end of Michigan Street, where Katherine (now Douglas) Street would later separate it from the park, the Munro home was sunny, spacious, and commanded a fine view south and east toward Beacon Hill. As the years went by and the park was developed, a walk to the Dallas Road cliffs led past Goodacre Lake and the western curve of the racetrack that circled the base of Beacon Hill. On the opposite side, other fine homes lined the road to the sea.

The Munro residence quickly became a social centre. Three daughters and four sons created a lively household, and their parents loved to entertain. All the Munro girls were married at the family home. In 1875, eldest daughter Elizabeth married local businessman Robert Paterson Rithet. Two years later, Mary married real estate whiz James Keith Wilson. In 1883, youngest daughter Jane married Captain John Irving of the Canadian Pacific Navigation Company.

Munro eventually took over management of the HBC's western operations. In 1890 he retired from the position of senior chief factor and went on to live contentedly for almost 21 years at his Michigan Street home. Eventually, in the first decade of the new century, he began to fail. He succumbed to a chest infection at

A few blocks from Munro's mansion, the grassy slope in front of the Birdcages
afforded this 1860s view north across the first James Bay Bridge, built in
1859 to allow easier access to the then-new Parliament Buildings.

the end of February 1911, at the age of 87. Three years later his wife Jane fell, fractured a hip, and died at the age of 89. The two are buried in the family plot at Ross Bay.

Today the students of South Park Elementary School play happily on the corner that was first claimed by this pioneer family. And in Esquimalt, where PSAC once reigned supreme, Munro Street crosses what used to be the southern part of Donald Macaulay's farm.

RITHET STREET

Businessman made his money on Wharf Street

*A*cross James Bay from Alexander Munro's home, son-in-law Robert Paterson Rithet changed the face of Victoria's shipping business with the construction of piers at his Outer Wharf. It was one of many highlights in a multifaceted career.

Rithet, born in Scotland in 1844, was not yet twenty when he decided to try his luck at mining Cariboo gold. It didn't take him long, however, to realize that his chances of success were greater in the newly incorporated city of Victoria than in the gold fields farther north. He settled there in 1862.

His rise to success began with his appointment as accountant to Sproat & Company. A hard worker, he quickly became adept at handling the business by himself during Gilbert Sproat's frequent absences. A promotion was in order, and in 1869 the 25-year-old Rithet was put in charge of the company's San Francisco affairs. It was one

Robert and Elizabeth Rithet

of the most important moves of his business career, because it introduced him to Sproat's business partner, Andrew Welch. Welch was a good role model and teacher, and Rithet was an eager student.

The mid-1860s brought disappointment to many of Victoria's merchants. It made sense from an administrative point of view to merge the two colonies of British Columbia (on the mainland) and Vancouver Island into one, but it meant that Victoria was no longer a free port, and talk of Confederation with the new Dominion of Canada was in the air. Many merchants, anxious to re-establish free trade with their neighbours to the south, lobbied for annexation with the United States. A few saw the advantages of leaving the border exactly where it was.

Rithet was one of the few. Undaunted by new directions and challenged by change, he epitomized a new breed of businessman—one who recognized

In the 1890s, R.P. Rithet & Company, wholesale merchants, shipping and insurance agents, was one of the city's largest employers. In the 1990s, the Rithet Building at 1117 Wharf Street housed the headquarters for provincial tourism, an industry that Rithet fostered a century earlier when he built his wharf at Ogden Point to accommodate ocean-going liners.

the positive aspects of the proposed measures and planned to profit by them.

Leaving Sproat & Company to work with J. Robertson Stewart, another well-established Victoria merchant, Rithet found himself managing the office when his employer became ill. Soon after, the business was put up for sale. Andrew Welch bought it and in 1870 renamed it Welch, Rithet & Company. When Andrew Welch died in 1888, Rithet bought out his interest and gave the company the name R.P. Rithet & Co.

Over the ensuing decades, the firm went from strength to strength. Starting with sugar trading with the Hawaiian Islands and importing groceries and liquor from all over the world, the company's interests expanded to involve lumber, sealing, whaling, canning, farming, shipping, insurance, mining, and railways. The wharf that Rithet built at Ogden Point just before the end of the nineteenth century made Victoria accessible to travellers aboard Canadian Pacific's ocean-going Empress liners.

Along the way, money made was ploughed back into local business ventures. Rithet was fast becoming a very wealthy man. He was also a family man, whose wife and children shared his good fortune.

Elizabeth Munro had sailed around Cape Horn with her mother and two sisters when she

The Rithet family home, called "Hollybank," was a wedding gift from Lizzie's father, Alexander Munro. Rithet's estate included all the land between Humboldt, Collinson, Quadra, and Vancouver streets. Part of the iron railing that once surrounded "Hollybank" can be found today behind the Royal B.C. Museum, surrounding a cherry tree planted by James Douglas in 1854 in what was then his garden. Douglas's house was demolished in 1906. "Hollybank" survived till 1953.

Rithet's farm north of the city—which, like his favourite stallion, was called Broadmead—is now a residential area.

The Rithet children, Jack (top left), Edward (who died young), and Gertrude, often walked from "Hollybank" across the north end of Beacon Hill Park to their grandparents' Michigan Street home.

when the tall, elegant Lizzie was 22 and Rithet was almost ten years her senior. Proud father Alexander Munro built a home for them on Humboldt Street, not far from his own.

"Hollybank," with its chandeliers, chimneys, tall windows, tennis courts, holly trees, and iron-fenced garden, was a stately residence for Rithet, Lizzie, and their two children (a third child, Edward, died young). Behind the house there were stables and a paddock for the horses. The children often rode with their mother, and John (called Jack) and Gertrude had only a short distance to walk to their grandparents' Michigan Street home.

Rithet the business and family man was also a prominent public figure who had been appointed a justice of the peace by Lieutenant Governor Joseph Trutch in the early 1870s. The respect generated by his many business involvements and public spiritedness stood him in good stead when, in 1884, he entered politics for the first time.

As a candidate for the office of mayor, he campaigned vehemently for adequate drainage. His bid was successful; he became mayor in 1884. From 1894 to 1898 he served as member of the legislative assembly for Victoria City.

Rithet was 75 years old when he died in 1919. Lizzie, who outlasted all her children, lived on at "Hollybank" into her 100th year and was buried beside her husband at Ross Bay in 1952.

Today the Rithets are remembered in Rithet Street in James Bay and by Rithet's Bog and Rithet Hill, just south of Royal Oak, where a suburban shopping centre—Broadmead—carries the name of Rithet's farm and his most famous Thoroughbred racehorse.

was five years old, bound for a new home and a joyful reunion with the father she had missed so much. As four brothers joined the growing family, the Munros moved to a new home beside Beacon Hill Park. It was here that Lizzie met the man she would marry.

Rithet first laid eyes on Elizabeth Munro when she was just sixteen. They married in 1875,

Steamboat captain sailed to success

Even when they married, Alexander Munro's daughters didn't stray far from home. Lizzie and her family lived just across the top of Beacon Hill Park, while Jane and the dashing Captain Irving lived a few blocks to the west on Michigan Street.

John Irving was born in 1854, the latest in a long line of Scottish adventurers. His father, a steamboat owner and master who had moved from Oregon to the Fraser River, made his money carrying gold miners from Yale to Hope. John grew up around boats. He had such a knack for sailing that by the age of eighteen he was

John and Jane Irving

navigating the Fraser's twists and bends, and at twenty he was a full captain—the youngest in the colony.

By that time his father was dead. John took over the Irving Pioneer Line and added more ships to it. From buying, he turned to building. His fleet included the *William Irving* (named

after his father) and the *Elizabeth Irving* (after his mother).

In 1882 Irving became manager of the Canadian Pacific Navigation Company. He was one of this town's most eligible bachelors—until he married Jane Munro. Jane was the youngest Munro girl and the last to leave the family home. She and Captain John were married at the Munro residence in June 1883, and a year later they moved into a grand home halfway across the James Bay peninsula.

In the 1850s and 1860s, James Bay was sparsely populated, taken up mostly with farmland and forest, but by the 1870s, much of Beckley Farm had been subdivided, and James Bay was a popular residential area. It was also somewhat exclusive, with the grandest homes flanking the Parliament Buildings that stood on the grassy slope by the Inner Harbour.

The Irvings' many-coloured mansion dominated the southwest corner of Menzies and Michigan streets in fashionable James Bay. The brickwork on the lower sections was painted in four shades of red. The upper portion was a mixture of olive green and seven other shades, while the roof copings, mouldings, and ornamental railings were painted a rich brown. Today, huge sequoias mark what was the driveway entrance.

In the 1880s, Menzies Street from Belleville to Dallas was the setting for large dwellings. Closest to the Inner Harbour was "Fairview," built for an American sea captain and destined to be a temporary home for two generations of Dunsmuirs. A few blocks south, "Irving Place" stood at the corner of Menzies and Michigan, its bay-windowed corners and porches guarded by California sequoias standing like sentries at both entrances to the curved driveway.

The mansion at 73 Menzies Street was a sight to behold—not just because of its size, but also because of its colours. People came from miles around to admire the reds blended with browns and greens; it was said there were twelve different shades. From basement brickwork to ornamental roof railing, imaginative paintwork picked out every cornice and cranny, and created what the *Colonist* in 1888 described as "a most pleasing appearance."

In 1891 the Irvings were the talk of the town again. This time it was their new phaeton carriage, built to order in Victoria for the captain's wife. She and her children were objects of admiration as they rode around the town, visited the children's grandparents, or went to Ogden Point to welcome their father home from one of his many sojourns at sea.

Running a successful business from behind a desk didn't appeal to the dashing captain; he wanted to be in the thick of things. He set up a Victoria–New Westminster steamboat service in direct competition with the Hudson's Bay Company and eventually bought out the

The William Irving *(shown here), named after John Irving's father, and the* R.P. Rithet, *named after the man who married John's sister-in-law Lizzie, formed part of a large fleet of steamships that plied the waters between Victoria and the mainland port of New Westminster.*

company's line. His Canadian Pacific Navigation Company was joined by the Yukon Navigation Company, created to profit from the Klondike gold rush, and the Columbia–Kootenay Navigation Company, which serviced the Kootenay River and adjoining Interior lakes.

The Yukon operation was later sold to the White Pass Railway. The CP Navigation Company and Interior lake operations, sold to the Canadian Pacific Railway in 1901, were destined to form the basis of that company's famous Princess line. The terms of the sale included a lifetime pass on CPR ships for Captain Irving, a privilege much enjoyed by him in later years, when his interests had turned to mining and politics.

In retirement, Irving started to spend more time in Vancouver and died there in 1936, aged 82. Jane went to England, where she died in 1950. They were survived by daughters Genevieve and Elizabeth. A son, William, had been killed in World War I.

Irving Road in Fairfield is actually named for Justice Paulus Irving, a former deputy attorney general, but the grassy area with the playground on the southwest corner of Menzies and Michigan is known as Irving Park in memory of the captain and his family. Giant sequoias mark either end of the drive that once led to the family home—a reminder of the father and son who made their fortunes in those far-off steamboat days.

GOVERNMENT STREET

You could bank on it

*L*ike other successful businessmen, Captain John Irving would have conducted financial transactions on Victoria's busiest thoroughfare. For storing and spending money, there was no place like Government Street. You could bank on it.

Government wasn't the only street to boast a bank, but it was the street that had the most. In those days the downtown core started at Johnson Street and ended at James Bay, and at one time several major banks operated within those few short blocks.

Government Street, the first paved street this side of the Rockies, was so named because when the Hudson's Bay Company established a presence on Vancouver Island in the 1840s, the seat of government was at the northeast corner of Fort Victoria. Government Street was the road that ran along the eastern boundary of the fort.

More than a decade later, three years before Victoria became a city, there wasn't a single bank in sight. Government Street was still a dirt road with a planked sidewalk, dry and dusty in summer, muddy in midwinter. Money was hard earned and soon spent. No one in this sleepy burgh had need of a bank.

Then, starting in the spring of 1858, Government Street was filled with prospectors headed for the mainland. Money changed hands in payment for supplies, and the miners went off to the gold fields. Many came back empty-handed and destitute; some returned with riches and to spare.

What do you do with gold dust? Carrying it around was too risky. Leaving it where you lived was less than smart. Sending it somewhere was asking for trouble. What you needed was a place to store your stash so you could sleep at night. A place that would lock it up and watch over it while you slept. In short, a bank.

Before long, five downtown firms were competing for the gold miners' business. Some even followed the miners north along the Fraser River and up into the Cariboo. Each mining town had bank branches. Gold was bought from the miners, then transported back to Victoria via stagecoach express.

One of the first fellows in Victoria to cash in on the money-making business was Alexander J. Macdonald. A canny young Scot, Macdonald had honed his craft in California. His bank on lower Yates Street, near Wharf, was built in 1859 to cater to the gold miners' needs. At last, thought the miners, their hard-earned gold was in good hands. Or was it? In 1864 a mysterious unsolved robbery brought Macdonald's bank to

Looking south along Government Street from Pandora toward James Bay in 1899, planked sidewalks are still evident, shades and awnings protect against the hot sun, and it's safe to jaywalk. In the distance, on the right, the Bank of Montreal's steep roof can be seen. By the turn of the century there were no fewer than eight different banks along Government Street between Humboldt and Yates.

its knees. Dismayed by the bank's apparent lack of security, depositors closed their accounts. Macdonald slid across the border and was never seen on these shores again.

Fortunately for his customers, Government Street's financial institutions enjoyed a better reputation, were well equipped to pick up the slack, and were more impressive to boot. In time-honoured tradition, banks did their best to look solid and dependable. Looking up at any one of those imposing structures, you could feel confident that your money was in good hands.

Right smack bang in the middle of all the activity was a fine brick edifice that had once belonged to Victoria's first mayor. Thomas Harris, elected in 1862, decided to remove his family to a quieter location nearby. Part of his motivation may have been the opportunity to rent his home on the corner of Government and Bastion streets to a bank owned by a

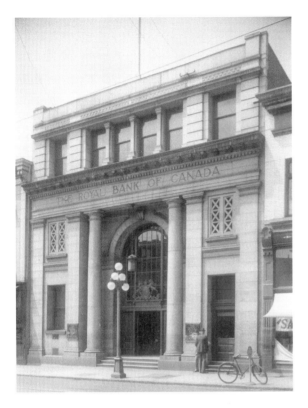

Formerly part of the building belonging to J.J. Southgate and H.D. Lascelles, the Royal Bank opened its doors to customers at 1108 Government Street in 1909. Its Temple Bank style, solid structure, and classic columns inspired customers to leave their money in the bank's safekeeping. Minus its original second storey, but retaining other external features, the great banking hall was preserved during interior renovations by bookstore owner Jim Munro in 1985.

The Francis Rattenbury-designed Bank of Montreal featured Haddington Island stone and the chateau style the architect would use again ten years later for the Empress Hotel. When it was erected in 1897 at the northwest corner of Government and Bastion streets, this building effectively blocked the direct sight-line from the east toward the harbour and is the reason why View Street doesn't have a view.

London group that had recently received a Royal Charter.

The first resident manager, arriving with three assistants in July 1862, negotiated successfully with Harris for a five-year lease and a monthly rental of $250. Within a year the bank had changed its name to the Bank of British Columbia and was issuing its own money—five-dollar bills printed on good paper and bearing the manager's signature.

Twenty years later the bank had outgrown the old Harris home. In 1885 it opened for

The seven-storey Union Bank (at left) and Central buildings dominated the northeast corner of Government and View streets in 1913. The bank, which opened for business in 1912 right opposite the Bank of Montreal, featured white glazed terra cotta corner blocks and window surrounds, and looks almost the same today as it did all those decades ago.

business in a new building on the southwest corner of Fort and Government, on the former site of the first legislative assembly at Fort Victoria. This building would eventually be used by the Canadian (later Canadian Imperial) Bank of Commerce, which purchased the Bank of B.C.

Harris's old home was demolished. In its place, in 1896, the chateau-style roof of the Bank of Montreal dominated the skyline. It was designed by Francis Rattenbury, the young architect whose Parliament Buildings were at

that moment taking shape on the other side of James Bay.

In the middle of the next block, on the same side, stood the Royal Bank. Established in 1869 as the Merchants Bank of Halifax, its first Victoria branch opened in 1898. In 1901 it became the Royal Bank of Canada.

Today, Government Street bears little resemblance to its beginnings as Victoria's banking centre. Gone are the planked sidewalks and the hitching posts where teams

The new headquarters of the Bank of British Columbia, which later amalgamated with the Canadian Imperial Bank of Commerce, was the largest office building in the province when it was erected in 1885 on the former site of the first legislative assembly's meeting place in Fort Victoria. Pictured here in 1913, it stands on the southwest corner of Government and Fort to this day, minus its fancy topknots but otherwise remarkably intact. Like other banks along the street, its interior has been altered to house a retail store.

were tied up while customers conducted business inside. Gone are the overhangs, thoughtfully provided by merchants to protect shoppers from the elements.

The bank buildings of Government Street are mere shadows of their former selves, facades recognizable and carefully preserved, but interiors changed to accommodate new tenants and new activities. They stand as mute, magnificent reminders of the city's early days.

CAMPBELL'S CORNER

He cornered the news

*I*n the Victoria of days gone by, Government Street had it all—food stores, furniture, general supplies. Money was made, money was spent. For security, you could bank on the banks. For a good time, you could visit one of several saloons. And for the latest news, you could count on "Campbell's Corner."

Francis Henry (Frank) Campbell had no idea when he landed here that his name would eventually go down in history. It was August 1858 and his focus was on the fortune to be made over on the mainland. He had an adventurous spirit, probably inherited from parents who brought him from County Tyrone, Ireland, to Philadelphia when he was just two years old, then moved him to Iowa a year later.

In 1852, when Campbell was twenty, gold rush excitement in California was at its peak. He crossed the Isthmus of Panama with barely a dollar in his pocket and headed for San Francisco, certain of sudden wealth. He achieved

Frank Campbell

only modest success. Six years later, still full of youthful exuberance, he followed his fellow gold seekers to the new El Dorado—the Fraser River.

He had married an Irish girl, Margaret Morrow, shortly before leaving San Francisco. Victoria was to be the first stop on their journey through life. In fact, it proved to be their last.

The Campbells stayed here a week, then sailed to the mainland. Over the winter he investigated business opportunities and checked out the mining prospects. They were not good. The Fraser had proved disappointing. The Thompson was not much better; the gold was fine but not plentiful enough to be a paying proposition.

Campbell considered his options. He could stay where he was, go back to San Francisco, or follow a fellow by the name of Sewell P. Moody to San Juan Island.

There was gold on that island, it was said.

Campbell and Moody paddled over in a canoe. There was no gold, only two groups of

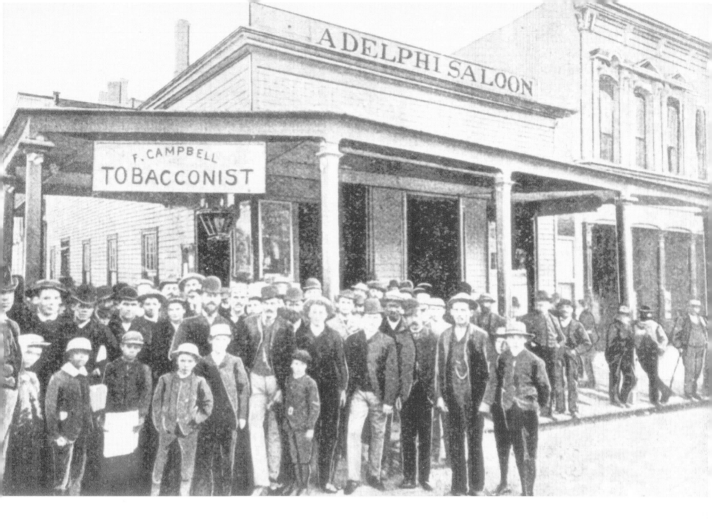

Frank Campbell cornered the news and tobacco business at Government and Yates Streets on the site of the first governor's residence in Victoria. The swinging doors of the Adelphi Saloon opened to the street on either side of Campbell's Corner, so customers exiting the saloon swung right into his store. Pictured here in the 1870s, Campbell's Corner was a focus for both locals and visitors who wanted the latest news.

people prepared to go to war over a wandering pig. Disappointed and disillusioned, Moody went back to the mainland where, decades later, his name was given to the settlement that later became the city of North Vancouver. Campbell moved to Victoria.

A carpenter by trade, he had no trouble finding work in the busy town, but soon struck out on his own, opening a general store on Johnson Street. A few months later he left Margaret minding the store while he chased gold again, this time in Leechtown, near Sooke. The Leech River find was another disappointment.

Campbell returned, determined to expand his business and make it pay.

First step was to focus his energies on one very popular product: tobacco. Second step was to sell it from a more central location. He walked up Johnson Street, turned right on Government, passed Thomas Harris's meat market in the direction of the harbour, and stopped at the next intersection. There it was. The perfect spot.

The corner of Yates and Government was at the heart of all the business activity. On the southwest corner stood the Adelphi Saloon, a one-storey building with access from both

In the 1890s, the southwest corner of Government and Yates still boasted a "Tobacconist" sign as Frank Jr. struggled to keep his father's business going. But there was nobody quite like genial, hard-working Frank Sr., the "King of Campbell's Corner" for more than 25 years. Eventually Campbell's store and the Adelphi Saloon were demolished and replaced by a post office, and later a federal government building.

streets. Before long it boasted a novel addition. Nestled between the two entrances, right on the corner, was Campbell's tobacco store.

The saloon's swinging doors ensured a constant flow of people. Few came and went without a visit to the store. Campbell was a genial host, always ready with a smile and a friendly word. Outside his door was a large bulletin board on which he tacked the latest news—snippets from the *Colonist*, reminders about coming events, notice of a marriage, or news of the imminent arrival of the mail steamer from San Francisco. He quickly earned an enviable

reputation. "It must be true," people would say, "because I saw it on Campbell's board!"

His newspaper advertisements were often in rhyming verse. A poem on the back of his business card read, in part:

> While in town you may be stopping,
> At the "Adelphi Corner" drop in;
> Campbell you'll find at that location,
> Ready to give you information,
> Or to see you well provided,
> With what is by all decided,
> The smoker's or the chewer's glory,
> The best and cheapest in all Victoria.

It was said that no other man in British Columbia could have made a better success of that corner. For almost 25 years Campbell operated the store from early morning till ten at night. Frank Jr., second of Frank Sr. and Margaret's four children, joined him in the family business. Of the girls—Virginia, Clara, and Martha—Martha was best known for her musical abilities, being the organ player in St. Andrew's Cathedral.

Life at the Campbells' home on Johnson Street, near Blanshard, was good. But sadness struck when Margaret, who suffered from kidney disease, died suddenly the day after Christmas 1888. For the first time in its history, the tobacco store stayed closed while the family mourned. Little more than two years later, "Genial" Frank Campbell was gone too, laid to rest beside his wife at Ross Bay Cemetery.

Campbell's Corner. Once, it was the place where Victorians gathered to gossip and discuss the events of the day. Today, no trace of it remains. A modern structure stands in its place, and there's no one left to remember the ruddy-faced Irishman who supplied tobacco, top news, and tips to the citizens of his day.

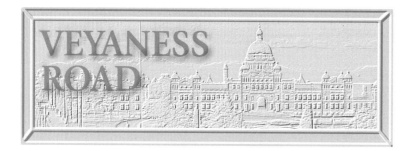

The Victoria & Sidney Railway

*I*n 1886, the hottest news item on Campbell's Corner was the talk of a rail link from Victoria to the mainland via the Saanich Peninsula. Its strongest supporter was Amor de Cosmos, one-time editor of the *Colonist*, former premier of B.C., and now Victoria's member of the Canadian parliament. De Cosmos wasn't the first to propose a link. That honour went to Mr. Arthur Bunster, a provincial politician in 1879.

The railway proved a hard sell. Bunster's plan was pooh-poohed; de Cosmos's scheme bit the dust; but others were more successful. By the 1890s all agreed that a railway line through the Saanich Peninsula was inevitable. It was just a question of who would build it, and who would benefit the most.

In the end it was clear that the gains would be shared by everyone—farmers and merchants in the newly developed township of Sidney, who

needed a faster route to the city for their products; residents of several settlements along the way; and the citizens of Victoria, who would have readier access to produce and fuel. By the early summer of 1892 the Victoria and Sidney Railway (V&S), whose directors included interested parties at both ends of the line, was incorporated. Surveying and construction began some months later.

If it's difficult now to imagine steam trains wending their way up and down the peninsula, it was difficult then for anyone to envisage sections of Saanich as anything but uninhabitable. Both ends of the peninsula boasted civilization, but in between there was only thick forest, scattered settlements, and a few farms. The sole route from Victoria to Sidney was by sea. Every Tuesday morning the *Isabel* left Victoria, sailed up the east coast of the peninsula and

Arthur Bunster (left) and Amor de Cosmos were early supporters of a Saanich Peninsula railway.

Engine No. 2, nicknamed "Deuce," shown here at Sidney Station, was the V&S's pride and joy, but it was daunted by heavy grades and, because it had no air brakes, was difficult to handle at station stops. Built in 1875, Deuce saw service in the Kootenays before being purchased for the Victoria–Sidney line.

round the top, and continued on up to Nanaimo and Comox. The 140-mile journey took two full days.

The V&S surveyors faced a daunting task, although it didn't seem so at the start. The first route they planned was practical. It made a beeline from one end of the peninsula to the other, followed plains and flatlands, and met with the approval of all except the residents in between, who were left high and dry.

An amended survey solved the problem. South of Sidney (for that's where the survey began) the line followed the coast to Bazan Bay, then veered west to Saanichton and south to Keating, weaving along the western side of Beaver and Elk lakes on its way to Royal Oak and, eventually, Victoria.

Even this route had its detractors. A trestle crossing the south end of Beaver Lake ran the risk of polluting the city's water supply, they said. The line should be moved farther over.

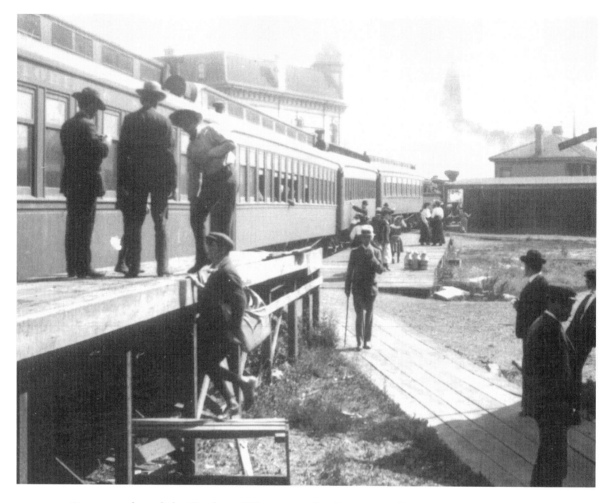

Passengers board the Cordwood Express at the downtown depot on Cormorant Street for the 50-odd-minute journey to Sidney in 1905. The Masonic Hall looms above the train. This part of Cormorant Street is now Centennial Square.

Eventually, yet another survey satisfied all the stated requirements. It wouldn't be long before its deficiencies became apparent, but in the meantime, Victoria looked forward to state-of-the-art travel in the twentieth century.

Clearing and grading started in September 1893. Supplies came by sea, and the track was laid from Sidney on down the peninsula. Everything proceeded according to plan until it reached a point about a mile north of the terminus. A large brickyard stood just about

where the Mayfair Shopping Centre is today, and a dispute with its owners caused some delay.

The line reached its temporary terminus at Tolmie Avenue, in the country north of Victoria, in March 1894. Two months later, a train heading north carried passengers bound for the North and South Saanich Agricultural Association's annual ball. According to the *Colonist*, those first travellers, who had previously faced a long journey by boat or along wagon trails, were deposited at their destination

When the V&S morning train pulled out of Victoria's Market Building Station (north side of today's Centennial Square), it moved east along Fisgard past the Masonic Hall, crossed Douglas (shown here, looking north on Douglas), and steamed one block east before turning north en route to Sidney.

Delays along the V&S route meant passengers often reached the Sidney wharf too late to catch the Strathcona, *which kept to a stricter schedule for sailings to the mainland.*

in good time and in good shape to dance the night away.

The first official run along the sixteen miles of track took place in July. A garland-and-flower-bedecked train transported special guests from Tolmie Avenue to Sidney in half an hour and returned them after suitable celebrations later in the day. All agreed that the railway was a resounding success.

It was fuelled by cordwood, so they called it the Cordwood Express, but in truth the new link between north and south was laid-back, even lethargic. The loads were heavy and the grades were steep, which often made the train late. Travellers thanked heavens for watering holes along the way!

In the early 1900s the line was taken over by the Great Northern Railway, but midway through the first decade, trains and terminals were displaying signs of disrepair.

By 1912, competition had surfaced in the form of the interurban B.C. Electric Railway, which ran up the western side of the peninsula along Interurban Road. A year later, the Canadian Northern Pacific Railway built a line from Victoria along Canora Road to Patricia Bay.

The Cordwood Express was also bedevilled by bad weather. The "Big Snow" of February 1916 brought it to a grinding halt. One train got stuck in the snow near Saanichton and had to back up all the way to Sidney. It was more than a week before a northbound train managed to push through from Victoria. Mail finally had to be sent the old way—by sea. A year later, when winter snows piled up again, the V&S was ready, but it would take more than surviving a snowstorm to save it. There was no way to compete with other carriers. There was no money for repairs. The Cordwood Express was coming to the end of the

The Cordwood Express struggled valiantly to beat the Big Snow of February 1916, but was brought to a grinding halt. By 1917, with the company a year older and wiser, the train managed to push through an equally severe storm. The snow cleared, but the Cordwood's biggest threat—increasing competition from other carriers—remained.

line. At the end of April 1919, after one last journey, the V&S went into receivership and became part of Victoria's history.

Today's Veyaness (Ve-yan-ess) Road follows the route of the old Victoria to Sidney line. With the help of George Hearn and David Wilkie's book *The Cordwood Limited* and Darryl Muralt's *The Victoria and Sidney Railway*, let us relive those days of steam. In the next few pages we'll take a trip on the old V&S, with some stops of interest along the way.

In 1914, huge sections of the Saanich Peninsula were still sparsely populated. The V&S connected Victoria with outlying communities, benefiting farmers and city-dwellers alike, and providing Gulf Island and up-Island passengers with speedier access. The route of the B.C. Electric Railway Interurban line is also visible in this illustration.

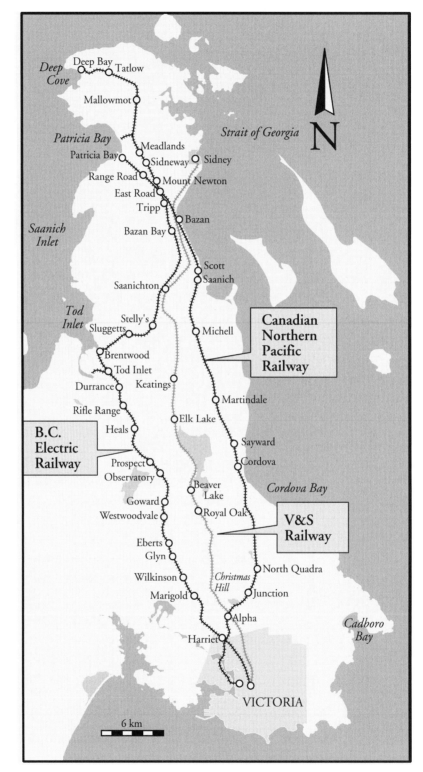

This map shows the stops on the three Saanich Peninsula rail lines.

CHRISTMAS AVENUE

The miracle of Christmas

For most of us, Christmas comes but once a year, but for the residents on one Saanich street, the festive season is a permanent fixture in their lives. The street was named for a racehorse called Christmas, owned by the same fellow who owned Midgard and Kisber. And a few kilometres almost due west of Christmas Avenue, just short of the old V&S Railway route, there is a place called Christmas Hill.

Christmas Hill, or Lake Hill as it once was known, is the first major "lump" due north of the Inner Harbour. Smaller than Mount Newton, gentler than Mount Tolmie, with smoother contours than Mount Douglas, Christmas Hill, like its companions, is a relic of the glacial age. Today it rises roundly above a modern housing development, but once it loomed above lush farmland. When Kenneth McKenzie left his job as bailiff at the Puget's Sound Agricultural Company's Craigflower Farm in the 1860s, he retired to Lake Hill's sunny southern slopes. Thirty years later, when the Cordwood Express lumbered away from the Victoria terminus and headed north toward Sidney, the hill was the first one encountered along the route.

The fact that its name is recorded on early Admiralty charts leads some to suppose that Christmas Hill was named for the day it was first climbed. But as numerous writers have recorded, there's another side to the story of Christmas Hill—a long-ago legend that persists to this day.

In the early days, when Fort Victoria was the centre of social activity in this area, Christmas was a fairly sober affair. Even after James Douglas became the fort's chief factor in 1849, the season was not celebrated with frivolity. Like any other fellow who'd spent his formative years in Scotland—and Fort Victoria boasted more than its fair share—Douglas knew that the *real* celebration was New Year, or Hogmanay.

For HBC contract workers, many of whom had wives and families back home, the holidays held little cheer. Far from being a celebration, the Christmas mood was melancholy. Relations between HBC men and local Natives were sometimes strained, at the least, and became near cordial at best as Christmas approached. But one year an event brought the two groups together in a way that no one could have planned ... or so the story goes.

It was Christmas Eve day. On the south shore of the Inner Harbour, where the legislature now stands, a Native child played near the water.

The Cordwood Express became a familiar sight along Rose (formerly First, later Blanshard) Street as it rolled sedately through the residential area north of town.

Her mother watched carefully, but she was totally unprepared for the danger that came, not from the water, not from the land that bordered it, but from above.

One minute the child was playing quietly; the next there was the sudden sound of beating wings. A large, black, raven-like bird swooped down from the sky and, while the young mother watched in horror, plucked the child from the water's edge and carried it aloft.

The mother was distraught. She cried out to others of her group and, almost hysterical with fear, pointed in the direction the bird had flown. While the women tried to comfort her, the men travelled north the only way they knew how— east along the shoreline to the place where the Church of Our Lord would one day stand, and across to the northern shore. As they walked, they called out to the missing child. Curious about the commotion, the men of the fort watched the group approach. When they heard

what had happened, they didn't hesitate. Lighting torches against the gathering gloom, they joined in the search.

The woman had pointed toward the north. The men left the modest comforts of the stockaded settlement and followed winding trails through the dense forest and swampland that lay north and east of the fort. Side by side, Native and newcomer, they watched carefully for any sign of life, calling out to the child and listening for a responding cry.

Now it was dark. They continued the search because no one wanted to face the anguished young mother who waited, weeping, in the harbourside camp. Hope had faded with the light, but still they pressed on. Circling Swan Lake, they moved ever farther from the fort, up the southern slope of the hill that loomed in the blackness. Slowly they climbed it, searching as they went. Tired though they were, and fruitless though it might seem, they didn't give

There was the child!

She was playing happily and was clearly unharmed. Tiredness forgotten, they scooped her up and retraced their steps to the fort. With relief, joy, and jubilation, she was placed safely in her mother's arms.

Some 50 years later, when the Cordwood Express rumbled along the track that bordered the east side of that hill, the fort was long gone and the festive season had become a joyful celebration. Christmas trees and gifts—all handmade—were enjoyed, but were not its main focus. The most important gift of all was family and friendship. Weeks before the Big Day, women made mincemeat for tarts, jams, cakes, and pies, as well as preserves and the plum pudding that would follow the turkey at Christmas dinner. Men readied the sleighs, groomed the horses, hunted wild game, gathered wood for the fire, and handcarved toys for their children.

Over the decades, the hill was chosen by the Chinese community as a burial site, farmed by a succession of landowners, and revered by a handful of retirees. At one point, Christmas Hill became Lake Hill, but eventually it was known as Christmas Hill once more because, no matter how improbable the story, no one ever tires of the tale of a child who was lost—and found again—on Christmas Day in the morning.

The station at Mark's Crossing at the north end of Elk Lake, pictured around 1904. The original V&S track-laying plans, which included a trestle across the southwest corner of Elk Lake, had to be revised because of fears that the city's water supply might be contaminated. Between stations there were less formal stopping places, like the one shown above, where the train stopped when necessary.

up the search. Every tree was examined, every bush was carefully checked.

It was hard to admit defeat, but when dawn broke, the truth could not be denied. A small human creature was no match for the bitter cold of a winter's night. All hope now gone, the men climbed wearily to the top of the hill, thinking to take stock of their surroundings and plan an alternative return route, when …

Second stop on the railway line

A short distance north of Christmas Hill, the original second station along the V&S route was Royal Oak. Apart from being the first scenic stop, Royal Oak Station—and particularly the nearby hotel—was a welcome sight for passengers and crew alike.

In the early days, the southern terminus of the Victoria & Sidney Railway was located at Nanaimo and Market streets, just north of Hillside Avenue. Later, the line originated closer to the city centre, which was much more convenient for passengers. The Victoria Market Building, on the north side of today's Centennial Square, seemed like the perfect spot for a railway station. Unfortunately it turned out to be not such a perfect spot for a railway. From a standing start, the locomotive had to struggle up the steep grade of Fisgard Street, across Douglas, and on up to Blanshard, where a sharp left turn put it on a northerly heading.

It became clear that the easiest way to lessen the strain on the locomotive was to avoid the Fisgard Street grade. Trouble was, although everybody agreed in principle, there wasn't a landowner in the area willing to lose a portion of his property. Eventually an agreement was reached with the City of Victoria, and just before Christmas 1910, the Victoria Market Station was relocated east, to Blanshard. From here the train could chug directly north, providing a faster and supposedly more efficient link between the city and the top end of the peninsula.

There were two trains a day from both terminuses on weekdays, with extra trains on high days and holidays. The journey from one end to another was scheduled to take 50 minutes, and a round-trip ticket cost 50 cents.

Of course it didn't always work out that way. The Cordwood Express had many supporters and just as many detractors, who snorted derisively when it had to back up and make several runs at the Royal Oak Hill. But love it or laugh at it, the railway was a boon to settlements along its route and was remembered fondly in later writings by many an early resident.

The train dropped off mail and daily papers, previously transported by stage. Farmers would separate their milk, then leave the large cans of cream for pickup by the train and delivery to the creamery near Victoria. Empty cans were returned later in the day. The Victoria Market terminus provided an outlet for fresh vegetables, dairy products, eggs, chickens ready for cooking, flowers and plants, fresh meat, home-cured ham and bacon, home-baked goods, jams, jellies, pickles, and preserves. People came from Sooke,

After years of once-a-week mail delivery by stage, peninsula residents were able to enjoy more frequent service. Six times a week, the V&S picked up and delivered mail to Royal Oak, Keating (shown here in a 1905 sketch by Lindley Crease), Saanichton, and Sidney.

Metchosin, Langford, Colwood, East and West Saanich, Cordova Bay, Cedar Hill, Cadboro Bay, and Gordon Head, knowing that they would have access to the fresh, high-quality products.

And always, on the train ride back home, there would be the journey through Royal Oak. Originally Station No. 2 on the line, Royal Oak was now Station No. 3. But the numbers didn't change the fact that it was a long haul up the Royal Oak Hill for the little wood-burning locomotive. Fortunately for the passengers, relief was in sight. Not far from the station was the Royal Oak Hotel. Legend has it that when a particularly heavy load slowed the Cordwood to a crawl, passengers would leave it at the foot of the hill and watch from the windows of the

hotel lounge as it struggled up the steep grade.

This was the second Royal Oak Hotel. The first had been built in the mid-1850s by Richard and Jane Cheeseman, who cleared land near where the trail from Victoria forked—the beginnings of West Saanich and East Saanich roads (this first section of East Saanich is now part of Viewmont Avenue). In 1873, Louis Duval, a recent arrival from Quebec via the Cariboo, bought the Royal Oak Hotel, and a few years later he was living there with his wife Janie, the Cheesemans' third daughter.

When it burned down some twelve years later, Duval built a second hotel at the same site. It opened for business in 1890, and over the years, many travellers on the trail to and from

Cutting diagonally, from right to left across the centre of this photo, the Cordwood Express steams south to Victoria through lush farmland. The steep grade at Royal Oak was an ongoing challenge on the Victoria-Sidney route, and the Royal Oak Hotel (seen in the distance above the V&S locomotive) provided a welcome watering-stop for northbound passengers.

In 1908, in an attempt to improve service, the V&S loaded the Royal Oak Station onto a flatcar and moved it north to Keating Cross Road (above). After numerous stops to clear the sides of the track to accommodate the extra-wide load, the train finally reached Keating. Much to the consternation of its regular passengers, the five-mile trip had taken the best part of a day.

Victoria were glad to see the lights of the hotel in the distance. By the time the Cordwood Express came chugging by in the mid-1890s, it provided a much-appreciated watering hole for parched passengers.

A decade or so later, the V&S decided to move the station farther north. It seemed like a fairly simple scheme—load the station building onto a flatcar and take it up to Keating Cross Road, where there were more potential customers. But unforeseen obstacles along the way included tree stumps, telephone poles, cattle guards, and even part of the station itself. The five-mile trip took all day. Passengers southbound from Sidney didn't get to Victoria till 10 p.m.—with no station-stop near the Royal Oak Hotel to help whet their whistles on the way.

Louis and Janie Duval

Railway stop in the heart of Saanich

Soon after the Cordwood left Royal Oak, it crossed Colquitz River and ran up alongside Beaver and Elk lakes. If the hill up to Royal Oak had been bad, this perilous part of the track was even worse because it had been relocated from its original proposed route to allay fears about water contamination.

One could understand the City Fathers' concern—after all, these lakes did supply Victoria's drinking water—but that didn't make life any easier for the V&S grading crew charged with preparing the land for a railway line. First they were laid off while the surveyors went back to the drawing board. Then they had the difficult task of laying track along a crest above the southwest corner of Elk Lake. But when they finished, their problems paled in comparison to the challenges faced by southbound trains forced to follow sharp, twisting curves over a muddy, unstable rail bed as they surged toward the summit north of Royal Oak.

One evening at the turn of the nineteenth century, those curves got the better of the Cordwood. Gathering steam for the pull up the steep hill ahead, the southbound passenger train came to a grinding halt when the weight of the train spread the track beneath its wheels and the train was derailed. The crew struggled to get the

locomotive back on track. The passengers walked the rest of the way (six miles) to Victoria. Inadequate drainage proved an insoluble problem, and unfortunately for the Cordwood, derailments were an all-too-frequent occurrence.

Once past the lakes on the northbound route, however, the Cordwood ran up to Keating, where the station at Royal Oak was eventually relocated, and on through lush farmland. Little more than half an hour after leaving Victoria, the train reached Saanichton.

There wasn't much to Saanichton in the mid-1890s—just a few buildings clustered near the corner of a rugged trail. This was Mt. Newton Cross Road, created some three decades earlier to connect West and East Saanich roads, the two equally rugged trails that ran north from the Duval's place at Royal Oak.

The land between these two trails was first settled in the 1850s by Angus McPhail, the Thomsons, and the Lidgates. Over the years these pioneers were joined by the Johns, Pridhams, Sluggetts, Wallaces, Popes, Andersons, Crawfords, Turgooses, and others. Near the crossroads junction there was a blacksmith's shop, a post office, and a building that later housed a general store. But when the Cordwood Express rolled into Saanichton, there

Richard Maynard took this picture of Beaver Lake in the 1880s, long before the Cordwood Express rumbled across its southern end. The original V&S route plan included a trestle running north-south across the centre of the lake. The track was subsequently relocated west onto the lakeshore.

was no more popular building for miles around than Henry Simpson's tavern.

In the days before the Cordwood connected the north end of the peninsula with the south, travellers followed the route on horseback or bumped and lurched along in wagons. Whichever way you arrived, the Prairie Tavern was a sight for sore eyes. Warm and inviting, it was just what the weary wanderer needed to help him on his way.

Simpson, who had farmed in the area since 1858, built the tavern a year later and opened it for business in 1864. In the late 1870s it became the headquarters for the area's first mail service. The enterprising postmaster had soon earned

Henry Simpson

enough to buy a coach that could carry several passengers as well as parcels.

Business was brisk, and about to get brisker. When Simpson learned that the proposed north-south rail link was going to run right past his front door, he knew exactly what he had to do. Leaving the Prairie Tavern where it was, he constructed another building beside it. By the time the Cordwood Express steamed into Saanichton on its inaugural run in April 1894, loaded with party-minded passengers, the new Prairie Inn stood ready to serve them. The Inn would continue to cater to locals and travellers long after Simpson (and the Cordwood itself) was gone, and it stands on the

All traces of the first tavern gone, Simpson's Prairie Inn (pictured here in the 1950s) stands on the corner of Mt. Newton Cross Road and East Saanich Road—the heart of Saanichton—to this day.

northwest corner of Mt. Newton and East Saanich roads to this day.

Twice a day, seven days a week, summer and winter, the Cordwood clattered along its route. Toward the end of the year it would carry extra loads on the northern run as passengers carried their Christmas purchases home. New Year's was a fairly quiet affair—staying up late isn't as tempting when cows must be milked before dawn—but Christmas was a joyous celebration. For the most part, Christmas gifts were of a practical nature and made by hand, but those who had saved a few cents could find bargains galore in town.

In December 1905 one Government Street jeweller tempted shoppers with silver thimbles, tie clips, and brass photo frames for 25 cents each, while 50 cents would buy you a silver shoehorn, ebony glove stretchers, or a comb. For 75 cents you could pick up a gold ring, a solid silver baby's rattle, or half a dozen teaspoons. Topping the "expensive gift" list were gold pens, whist markers, and jewelled brooches, at $1 each.

Bright lights beckoned. Coins burned holes in pockets. And at the end of the day, you could take your treasures home to Saanichton on the Cordwood Express.

One hundred years after the first Saanich settlers put down their pioneering roots, boys and girls of McTavish School, grades 4 to 6, found a unique way to record their names and locations. This tapestry (at right), which shows who lived where on the peninsula in 1874, is displayed at the Sidney Museum.

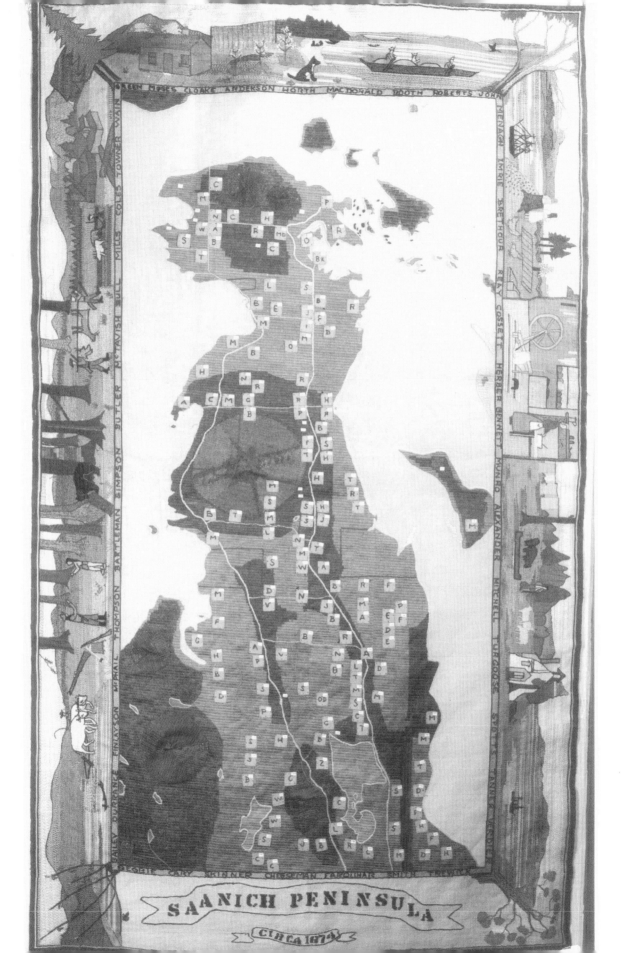

SAANICH PENINSULA

CIRCA 1874

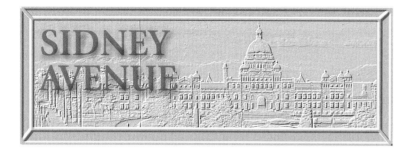

Brothers owned land at the end of the line

*L*eaving the inviting warmth of the Prairie Inn, the Cordwood had only four miles to go before the end of the line. This was the easy part. From Saanichton, it was just a hop, skip, and a rumble north through the prairie to the waterfront at Bazan Bay, and on up to Station 0 in the village of Sidney.

This area was originally home to people of the Coast Salish nation. For centuries they had lived on the waterfront in the bays to the north and south of what became a white settlement. Each spring they faced attack from marauding tribes from farther up the coast. At one point, after the Europeans arrived, their ranks were thinned by smallpox. Eventually they moved to a safer, more sheltered spot on the west side of the peninsula.

In 1858 the Hudson's Bay Company, intent on developing the Saanich Peninsula as a farming settlement, offered 100-acre parcels of land for sale. Many of them were snapped up by speculators and remained largely uninhabited for decades—no one wanted to live so far from town—until a family arrived and literally put this patch of land on the map.

Samuel Brethour arrived in Saanich by way of Ontario. His ancestors had left their native Germany in the 1700s and set sail for

New York. Their ship foundered off the coast of Ireland, and they stayed there for more than a century.

Samuel was sixteen when his parents decided to emigrate. They settled in Ontario, where Samuel married Margaret and fathered eleven children. In the early 1870s, the family travelled by train to San Francisco, then sailed up the West Coast.

Deciding in 1873 to settle on Vancouver Island, Samuel bought 500 acres of land just south of the Saanich Peninsula's northeast tip. His property stretched from the waterfront to a point west of the present-day Pat Bay Highway. Samuel, who was now in his 50s, enlisted his sons' help to clear the land and gave each one a parcel. He died in March 1877 and was the first to be buried in the family cemetery. Margaret, who fell sick after nursing their youngest son when he was stricken by typhoid, joined him there six years later.

Only one of Brethour's sons, John, had ever been seriously interested in farming. The others were more business-minded, and in 1891, Julius, Wesley, Henry, and Samuel Jr. incorporated their land and established a township. They called it Sidney, after the island directly to the east. Seeing the potential in the area, Julius invited an

Julius (left), Sam (centre), and Henry Brethour

acquaintance from Ontario to start a sawmill in the new town. With James J. White and his nephew at the helm, the Toronto and British Columbia Lumber Company quickly became a going concern.

When the Brethour brothers heard about the proposed railway line that would connect Sidney and Victoria, they were quick to react. Henry and Wesley had already donated land from First Street to the sea for the mill. Now Julius donated his waterfront property for a railway terminus. At the first meeting of the Victoria & Sidney Railway Company in September 1892, he became one of its first directors. Thus it was that when the Cordwood bounced along the Bazan Bay shoreline into Sidney on that sunny day in May 1894, it rattled over railway ties produced at J.J. White's mill and rolled right onto Julius Brethour's land.

By this time Sidney boasted a few scattered dwellings, several stores, a hotel, and a wharf. White wasn't the only one who profited from the presence of the railway. Thomas W. Paterson also did well. Paterson had extensive railway-building experience in the Interior and competed successfully to be contractor for the Cordwood. Once it was completed, he stayed on to become the company's general manager. He also had a contract to supply wood for the steam locomotive, which was stacked up in cords at the trackside. In the first six years of the Cordwood's operation, it guzzled enough of Paterson's wood to make him richer by some $13,000—a fortune in those days.

Unfortunately, while the GM was making money, the Cordwood was barely making the financial grade. Still it laboured on. It was a boon to passengers, providing the opportunity for excursions from Victoria to Sidney on sunny summer days. It was welcomed by weekend hunters, who gained easy access to game. Mail service, which Henry Simpson had started in the late 1870s, was much improved. Appreciative as well as enterprising, the newspaper boy was able to deliver the *Colonist* along the route from the early morning train and still make it back to Victoria in time for school.

The Cordwood provided an alternative for passengers bound up-Island. They could travel to Sidney by train, then catch a Nanaimo Navigation Co. steamer to the Gulf Islands and Nanaimo instead of having to sail all the way round from Victoria. On Saanich Fall Fair days, expanded service included an extra evening train that connected with the steamship *Iroquois* in time to take passengers on a moonlight cruise through the Gulf Islands.

Established by Samuel Brethour in 1873, the 500-acre "Janesville" farm covered all the land from east of the present-day Patricia Bay Highway over to the Sidney waterfront. In 1891, Samuel's four sons incorporated their land and established the township of Sidney.

But there were problems. For one thing, the Cordwood was almost never on time. Sometimes it was a late ferry connection at Sidney that kept the train at the northern terminus while passengers fumed and fretted farther down the line. Other times it was derailed, or it had to wait while cows were rounded up and milked before the cans could be loaded onto the train.

Despite the fact there was no dispatcher, next to no flagging, and only one telephone line to connect the Cordwood's operators, there was not a single collision. There were other mishaps, particularly at the northern end of the line. It was always a struggle, for instance, to get off the wharf at Sidney. The train might have to run forward, then back, several times before getting up enough steam to crawl up the track to join the mainline. The wharf was not lighted during the summer, so if the train was late, passengers had to climb down and clamber aboard the *Iroquois* in the dark.

The first passenger train rolled in to the Sidney terminus, built on land donated by Julius Brethour, in May 1894. Here, horses and buggies await arrivals on the northbound train.

The Brethour family held a reunion in the mid-1930s at J.J. White's Killarney Lake property.

The early 1920s were the best years for Sidney Mills (formerly J.J. White's Toronto and British Columbia Lumber Company), which had suffered many setbacks and economic slumps. The mill was the community's largest employer, providing work for more than 300 people before it was forced to close during the Great Depression.

All in all, though, it was a whole lot better than the slow, uncomfortable journeys of days gone by. It just wasn't making any money. The addition of a second steamship on the Nanaimo run attracted extra traffic, but it still wasn't enough. Extension of the line south into the heart of Victoria didn't help. A direct connection with the mainland failed to produce the hoped-for increase in income. It didn't matter what they tried, the Cordwood was always more of a liability than an asset. Two new rail services on the

peninsula only served to point up the Cordwood's deficiencies, and in 1919 it ran for the last time.

It's hard to picture a steam train chugging up the peninsula today, but the people who played such a large part in the location of its northern terminus should not be forgotten. Next time you drive out to Victoria's bustling international airport, make a detour to the small cemetery surrounded by a high hedge that nestles on its eastern edge, and remember the Brethours, who founded a town called Sidney.

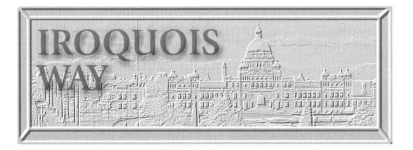

IROQUOIS WAY

Calamity off Sidney

*I*n 1871, one of the "carrots" dangled in front of British Columbia as an incentive to enter Confederation was a cross-country railway line. It was to start at the east coast and slowly but surely make its way west, putting an end to B.C.'s virtual isolation and joining it forevermore with the rest of Canada.

There was no question in anybody's mind that the logical place for a western terminus was Vancouver Island. Nanaimo made noises about its suitability as a terminus site. Victorians, ever conscious of their city's status as the capital of B.C., naturally assumed the line would end in Victoria. What a shock when news came that the western terminus was to be Vancouver—incorporated as a city 24 years after Victoria, but now selected for stardom!

Once they got over their disappointment, Victorians set to work to make their own connections for travellers and freight. People were settling on the Gulf Islands, north of the Saanich Peninsula, and others needed a faster, more direct route from Nanaimo to the capital. By 1895 the Victoria & Sidney Railway had connected Victoria and Sidney, eliminating the long—and sometimes dangerous in bad weather—voyage around the peninsula from Victoria by sea. Soon, steamers stitched island

to island and, eventually, Island to mainland, where freight and passengers transferred to a branch of the transcontinental railroad.

First link in this chain was the *Isabel*, which serviced the Gulf Islands route. The *Isabel* often anchored offshore, requiring passengers to row out to meet it. Then came the *Mary Hare*. This was the vessel that, in conjunction with the V&S, afforded excited Victorians the first railway and steamboat excursion to the Gulf Islands in June 1895. Smaller than the *Isabel*, the *Mary Hare* could pull into the most modest of docks to pick up whatever was waiting there. Before long, the *Victoria Times* announced that the steamer was bringing wool, sheep and lambs, dairy products, and fruit back from the islands, all destined for speedy delivery to the city centre on the morning train.

Sadly, this sterling service did not continue for long. One morning early in 1896, the *Mary Hare* struck a rock off Chemainus. All attempts to refloat the boat failed, and sometime in the evening, while captain and crew were enjoying a homecooked meal ashore, the *Mary Hare* caught fire and burned to the waterline. For the next four years, freight, mail, passengers, and anything else bound for the Gulf Islands was transported in small boats.

The Isabel, *pictured in Nanaimo Harbour, was the first of a fleet of steamers that provided an efficient sea link between the Saanich Peninsula, the Gulf Islands, and points up-Island.*

By the turn of the century it was painfully obvious that without its seagoing connection, the V&S was falling short of expectations and was losing money to boot. Early in 1900, a new V&S subsidiary, the Sidney and Nanaimo Transportation Company, was awarded a contract to carry mail to the islands. Freight and passenger service would also be reinstated. The vessel to be used was the brand-new *Iroquois*, at that moment being fitted with a boiler at a Victoria wharf.

The 20-horsepower, single-screw *Iroquois* was designed for island hopping. At 82 feet long, it could easily manoeuvre through coastal waters and was capable of transporting 40 passengers and 50 tons of freight at a top speed of 12 knots per hour. Some wondered if the boat's shallow draft would make it top-heavy in rough seas, but those fears faded into the background in the excitement of the inaugural run on April 2, 1900.

The *Iroquois* quickly became a firm favourite. Before long it was calling at more than twenty points along the route from Sidney to Nanaimo, delivering mail, carrying produce between the Saanich Peninsula and Gulf Islands, forming a valuable—and for delighted passengers, enjoyable—connection with Victoria via the V&S. Six days a week the *Iroquois* steamed out on the route. On the seventh day it rested, for alterations and repairs.

As the first decade of the twentieth century drew to a close, the *Iroquois* was joined by other vessels, which sailed to Nanaimo and plied the long-awaited route between Vancouver Island and the mainland. Still, when peninsula people wanted temporary respite from what were described as "the seductions of Government Street and the opportunities offered by a large town," the *Iroquois* provided the perfect escape. Sadly, the story has a less-than-perfect ending.

Soon after the Iroquois, *third ship in the steamship fleet, went into service in 1900, Sidney School pupils and teachers enjoyed a picnic cruise aboard her.*

SS Iroquois *was a welcome visitor to Salt Spring Island. Products picked up at Ganges could be in Victoria by the next morning.*

Pictured here between North and South Pender Islands on one of her regular twice-weekly runs through the area, the Iroquois *also provided regular return service to Nanaimo and points in between.*

It was April 10, 1911. By the time the northbound Cordwood Express reached Sidney, a strong southeasterly wind was already tossing the *Iroquois* about like a cork. The shallow hold was full and the deck was loaded with freight, including a large quantity of pig iron and several bales of hay. None of it was secured.

The seas kept throwing the *Iroquois* against the ferry dock. The passengers huddled hesitantly on the dock. At 9:10 a.m., anxious not to sustain further damage, the captain called for the stragglers to come aboard so the vessel could get under way. This was no worse than other journeys, he said. The *Iroquois* would weather it as before.

He was wrong.

The wind howled. First one huge wave battered the steamer, then another. With nothing to hold it in place but its own weight, the cargo shifted, and the ship listed. Before the captain could right it, and to the horror of those watching from the wharf, the vessel capsized and started to sink. Within minutes, it was gone.

The people watching from the shore were galvanized into action, running along the shoreline, putting out in boats, doing everything possible to save those who had not gone down with the ship. They worked tirelessly on into the night. Not until two days after the tragedy would the dreadful truth be known—21 dead or missing. Only four passengers survived. The six crew members who made it to shore included the captain. He was accused of manslaughter, but was later acquitted. His Master's Certificate was cancelled. He would never sail again.

Less than a decade later, the V&S was relegated to the pages of history.

Two women adorn the cowcatcher of V&S #1 locomotive as it sits on the Sidney dock.

An electrifying ride

For almost twenty years the Victoria & Sidney Railway reigned supreme on the Saanich Peninsula. Adored by children, but derided by many of their elders because of its unreliable schedule, the Cordwood Express held its own through the first twelve years of the 1900s. Provided you weren't in too much of a hurry, a railroad trip through the quiet countryside north of Victoria could be a delightful escape. The land was little changed from earlier years. Dense forest combined with gently rolling hills and lush green valleys to provide a veritable feast for tired eyes. The shrill whistle and steamy rumble of the railway made a pleasant change from the clanging clatter of streetcars on city streets.

The long-awaited ferry service to and from the mainland proved profitable. Tugs and barges crisscrossed the Strait of Georgia, connecting Vancouver Island with the Great Northern Railway terminus at Port Guichon, just south of Ladner. Freight and passenger business improved steadily. Despite setbacks such as the sinking of the *Iroquois*, the V&S seemed to have gained a new lease on life.

Then competition appeared in the form of another kind of railway. One that didn't have to pick up piles of cordwood along the track. One that ran on hydro-electric power.

Electric streetcars had been a feature of the Victoria scene since early 1890. In those days, automobiles were still the rich man's toy; a passenger hopping on or off a moving streetcar faced more danger from a horse and cart or a cyclist flying along the street at upwards of fifteen miles per hour.

The B.C. Electric Railway had made a huge difference on the mainland, where an interurban service running along the Fraser Valley had spurred an unprecedented increase in settlement along its route. Island realtors must have rubbed their hands with glee at the prospect of the land boom that promised to come their way.

From a modest beginning, Victoria and its streetcar service grew together. One line became two lines, then three, then four. Oak Bay, Uplands, Fairfield, Hillside, Richmond, Esquimalt, the Gorge, Burnside—all previously considered isolated—now were readily accessible. Sightseeing became the order of the day. Open excursion cars carried sightseers to areas rarely visited before. Residents and visitors alike enjoyed the new-found freedom of travel for a standard five-cent fare.

The streetcar operation went through several name and ownership changes—National Electric Tramway and Lighting Co., Victoria

Victoria's streetcar system began in a small way with a handful of open-ended electric trams like the one pictured above. Looking north on Government Street in 1900, the chateau-style roof of the recently completed Bank of Montreal building is at centre left. There is little traffic to impede the progress of the three well-dressed women crossing the Fort Street intersection. The streetcar approaching behind them is preparing to turn left up Fort on its way out to the Oak Bay terminus.

The laying of tracks for the Saanich line created a great deal of activity at Pandora and Douglas, where the streetcars veered west to join Interurban Road at the beginning of their journey up the peninsula.

Almost three years after the proposed Interurban line was announced in the
Colonist, a B.C. Electric Railway car, bedecked with ribbons and flags,
made its inaugural run up the Saanich Peninsula on June 18, 1913.

Electric Railway and Lighting Co., Consolidated Railway Co.—before becoming the B.C. Electric Railway Co. in 1897. This was just one year after the company's terrible disaster at Point Ellice, when the bridge collapsed under the weight of an overloaded streetcar, killing 55 people and injuring almost three score more.

In the early years of the twentieth century the BCER, buoyed by increased profits and encouraged by a surge in immigration, started to look farther afield. The V&S was in trouble. Despite the Island-mainland connection, profits were not rising as anticipated. Rolling stock was in need of repair. Trackage needed attention. The V&S ran up the centre of the peninsula, but the BCER saw routes on either side of it as fair game.

In 1912 the company started to build an interurban line from Victoria up the west side of the Saanich Peninsula. An extension of the Burnside line, it followed today's Interurban Road, heading north past Prospect Lake to Brentwood. Instead of carrying on along the coastline, the track swung across to Saanichton. From there it almost teasingly paralleled the V&S along Bazan Bay before veering west again toward Patricia Bay. Before reaching the bay itself, it turned and ran north to Horth Hill, then swung west to its terminus at Deep Bay, or Deep Cove as it is known today.

Construction moved at a fast pace. The line was completed a year later. No matter that it was way over budget; the V&S was going to get

*By the 1950s, the BCER tracks were long gone, but Interurban Road
(seen here looking north where it forks away from Burnside) was still a
quiet side-road leading away from the city towards Brentwood Bay.*

a run for its money. Thumbing its electric nose at its counterpart, the BCER laid a temporary interchange track, connecting with the V&S, alongside East Saanich Road at Saanichton. On June 10, 1913, the V&S suffered the indignity of delivering to its competitor the first two Interurban cars—one for passengers, one for baggage—which had arrived at the Sidney dock. Three days later the V&S closed the connecting line.

On June 18 the Interurban started its regular runs. Soon there were six round-trips a day. Fares were cheap—three cents per mile—and the one-way journey took just over an hour. Let's go for a ride on the B.C. Electric line!

Railway ran through Garden City

Sometimes it's interesting to wonder why some people *don't* have a Victoria street named after them, especially when they made a significant mark on the city's history. A good example of this phenomenon is Richard McBride—one-time premier of B.C. and promoter of the B.C. Electric Railway's interurban extensions on the Island.

McBride was born in New Westminster, B.C., of Irish parents, in 1870, one year before the province entered Confederation. He was schooled in New West, then studied at Dalhousie University and earned a law degree at the age of twenty. Returning to B.C., he was called to the bar in 1892 and became junior partner in a law firm. For the next thirteen years he practised in partnership or alone, and in 1905 he was named a King's Counsel.

McBride's political career had begun in earnest in 1896, with an unsuccessful campaign in the Dominion general election. Two years later he tried provincial politics and became MLA for Dewdney riding. In 1900, Premier

James Dunsmuir made him Minister of Mines. McBride resigned from cabinet a year later over a difference of opinion on policy and became leader of the opposition in 1902. In the 1903 election he took the provincial government's top post, becoming the sixteenth and, at 32, the youngest premier of British Columbia.

Margaret and Richard McBride

He was also one of the most popular. A tall, good-looking man with, by that time, a mane of prematurely grey hair, he was affable and engaging and had an incredible memory for names. He was also ambitious and shrewd, a fluent and articulate speaker who could make

Sir Richard McBride was surrounded by proud BCER officials
when he drove the last spike in the Interurban line at Deep Bay.

impromptu presentations at the drop of a hat. If he were called upon to speak on a subject about which he knew little or nothing, he would quickly find someone who knew more, then sprinkle his speech with enough information to impress and disarm his listeners.

These talents served him well. He had inherited a hornet's nest of working-class protest, fuelled by people in a province with no money. McBride took advantage of the recent intro-duction of the Worker's Compensation Act, assuring workers that shorter working hours and safer working conditions would soon be the order of the day.

McBride's ability to relate to all levels, to bring together all of the Conservative party's discordant elements and at the same time make working people believe he was one of them, sustained him through several terms. In 1907 and 1909 he was elected again. By the time the 1912 election rolled around, he was an old hand at campaigning. His speeches, previously effective despite their seeming lack of structure, were better organized and more concise. The crowds loved him. In this same year, King George V of England honoured him with a knighthood. He was invested with the insignia of the order of the Cross of St. Michael and St. George by the governor-general, the Duke of Connaught, in Victoria.

A faithful follower of the national party line, McBride was a fervent supporter of the B.C.

On June 18, 1913, McBride rode on one of the interurban cars (above) and
drove the last spike at Deep Bay (facing page) to celebrate the opening of the
new electric rail line from Victoria to the end of the Saanich Peninsula.

mainland's interurban railway and actively promoted an Island extension. In the tenth year of his premiership it became a reality. On June 18, 1913, McBride joined several other dignitaries on board a gaily decorated electric railway car downtown. Less than an hour later, when he drove a suitably inscribed silver spike into the ground at Deep Bay, the Interurban line to North and South (now Central) Saanich became a reality.

In 1896, the year of his first foray into politics, McBride had married Christina Margaret McGillivray at New Westminster. Moving to Victoria when he became premier, they lived for a while at Rupert and Heywood streets, then on lower Quadra, before buying a large house on the Gorge. "Glenela," built in 1908, had terraced gardens facing onto the waterway. It was a handsome home, with tall chimneys, a round tower at one end that afforded expansive views over the Gorge, and plenty of room for the dances the six McBride daughters loved to hold.

The BCER Interurban line that McBride had promoted so vigorously hummed along a few blocks away. From its southern terminus at Douglas and Pandora, the train ran along the existing Burnside streetcar line, then crossed Harriet and Tillicum not far from McBride's Gorge-side home, rolling through Matthias Rowland's farm and past his Burnside Hotel, built in 1884. Next stop: Marigold, where streets with names picked straight from an English

The McBride's home, "Glenela," pictured here from its entrance off Gorge Road, looked out over the Gorge waterway.

country garden hugged the line as it pushed its way up to the west side of the peninsula.

In the summer of 1914, McBride turned his attention to the war that loomed across the sea. There were enemy ships in the Pacific, and he quickly moved to protect his beloved province by purchasing two submarines. The Canadian government soon bought the subs from B.C.

The next year, McBride shocked British Columbians by suddenly leaving the premiership in favour of a post as B.C. agent-general in London. He was forced to resign in May 1917 due to ill health. By August he was dead, the victim of kidney disease at the age of 46. His family brought his body back to the Island, and he was buried at Ross Bay Cemetery.

At one time there were two streets called McBride—that portion of Blanshard Street between Queens and Bay, and an Oaklands street that now bears the name Victor. Now there are none. He was B.C.'s youngest premier, the first Conservative leader, the first to be knighted, and at that point the longest-serving premier. Elsewhere in the province, a lake, a river, a road in Prince Rupert, a mountain, and a central Interior town remind us of his name.

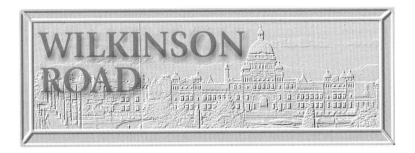

Jail and nursery bordered the line

Next stop on the Interurban line after Marigold—three minutes as the train flies—was Wilkinson. Wilkinson Road ran from Portage Inlet up to and beyond West Saanich Road. It was probably named after a family of farmers in this area, though there was also a Rev. Robert Wilkinson in the area, the pastor of the Methodist (now Christian Life) Church.

Just north of the railway track on Wilkinson stood a strangely familiar structure. It stands today, looking like a cross between a castle and a country home and bearing a marked resemblance to another structure at the corner of Bay and Blanshard streets. That similarity is not surprising, since the same man—Colonel William Ridgeway Wilson—designed both buildings.

What is commonly called the Wilkinson Road Jail has sported several different names over the years. In the beginning it was simply called Colquitz Jail, designed as a replacement for the old Victoria City Jail on the Topaz hill. Building began in 1912, one year before the B.C. Electric Railway extended its Burnside line.

The place the *Colonist* described as the Saanich Prison Farm didn't house former occupants of Topaz Jail for long. During the 1914-18 war, convicts were transferred to Oakalla Prison Farm in New Westminster, while Colquitz Jail became the temporary home of prisoners of war. After the war, renamed Colquitz Centre for the Criminally Insane, it eventually housed as many as 300 inmates. In 1964 the last of these was transferred to Essondale, on the mainland. Called Oakalla Prison Farm, Vancouver Island Unit, for several years, the building assumed its present official name—Vancouver Island Regional Correctional Centre—in 1971.

North of the jail's iron gates and distinctive stone wall was Rev. Wilkinson's church, completed in 1913 as the latest offshoot of the Methodist mission established in the area some 25 years before. Just beyond the church was the land belonging to Victoria's first nurseryman, Richard Emil Layritz.

Layritz was born near Dresden, Germany, in 1867, the son of a cloth manufacturer. The younger Layritz preferred making gardens. He studied in Stuttgart, Paris, and London, and when he learned about the opportunities to be had in the new country called Canada, he decided to leave the Old World behind.

Montreal was the nineteen-year-old's first stop in 1887. A year later he made his way across to the West Coast and settled on the spot with

Reverend Robert Wilkinson (inset) was pastor of the Methodist (now Christian Life) Church, not far from Richard Layritz's nursery.

the best climate for horticulture—Victoria, on Vancouver Island. He started a nursery in Fairfield, near the cemetery built on land once owned by Isabella Ross, widow of the first chief factor at the old fort. A freezing cold winter killed his plants, so he purchased an acreage out in the Saanich countryside, on the west side of the rough trail called Wilkinson Road.

Even with the willing help of local Natives, clearing the property of its tall trees took almost a year and most of Layritz's money. The next years were hard for Layritz—and for B.C., as the province entered a depression. It wasn't until 1898, when Layritz worked as a labourer in the

Klondike gold fields, that he earned enough money to return to Victoria a year later, pay off his debts, and begin again.

Now Layritz could afford to travel to California to buy clippings, cuttings, and sequoia seeds for his nursery. These eventually grew into plants and trees that graced Beacon Hill Park, the grounds of the Parliament Buildings, and the yards of private dwellings, and helped give his adopted home the nickname City of Gardens.

Layritz bought property in the Blenkinsop Valley, started nurseries in Gordon Head, then expanded his activities to include Vancouver and

*Pictured in the 1960s during its final days as Colquitz Mental Hospital, the former
Colquitz Jail—now the Vancouver Island Regional Correctional Centre—is surrounded
by fewer trees but retains its imposing, somewhat forbidding facade of days gone by.*

B.C.'s Interior. When the now-famous Okanagan orchards were developed, he was ready to supply their owners with fruit trees—an average of 40,000 for each 100-acre orchard.

Layritz was a hard worker, a short, slight man with strong hands and back. He rose at dawn and worked steadily till dusk in every kind of weather. Many of the trees that shaded Victoria's streets began as seedlings on Layritz's land. He grew ornamental shrubs, roses, and rhododendrons, shipping plants and cuttings to Washington, Oregon, Europe, and Asia. His name became synonymous with quality and integrity, and his reputation spread far and wide.

He was for several years president of the Pacific Northwest Nursery Association.

In the early days, Layritz lived a lonely life on Wilkinson Road with few close neighbours, but in 1906 he returned to Germany and married 21-year-old Eliese Vetter. He was eighteen years her senior. She was a lovely girl, well educated and a talented musician, who arrived in Victoria to find herself mistress of the simple home Layritz had built for himself in 1891. She was out of her element and missed the social life she was used to. By the time the B.C. Electric Railway started along its Interurban line, Mrs. Layritz was not long for this

Richard and his second wife Dorothy Layritz entertaining friends at their Wilkinson Road home.

world. She died in 1916, some say of a broken heart.

Three years later, Layritz married again. Dorothy was an English girl, a sturdier sort, who cared deeply for her husband and eventually outlived him.

In the 1940s Layritz donated ten acres of his land to Saanich for a park. Another five acres were added later. When he died in 1954, at the age of 88, his ashes were buried, at his request, under one of his beloved sequoias at what is now 4362 Wilkinson. Later Dorothy's ashes were buried there too. A plaque on the tree marks their final resting place. And a short distance to the south, off Glyn Road, Layritz Avenue and Layritz Place take you to the parkland that perpetuates the Layritz name.

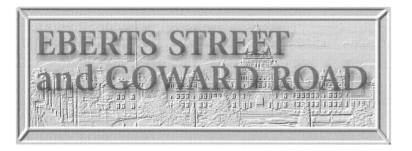

The politician and the railway manager

Several prominent personages involved with set-up and operations of the B.C. Electric are commemorated at different points along the line. Not far north of Wilkinson, one of these men—D.M. Eberts—lent his name to Stop No. 8. The other—A. T. Goward—was remembered at Stop No. 10.

David McEwen Eberts was born in Chatham, Ontario, in 1850. He studied law at Osgood Hall in Toronto before moving out to the West Coast in the late 1870s. In 1879 he was appointed a notary public, and the next year was called to the bar.

In the early 1880s Eberts started courting Mabel Charles, whose father, William Charles, was a prominent Hudson's Bay Company man. In June 1884 David and Mabel were married by Bishop George Hills at Christ Church Cathedral up on Church Hill (now Burdett Avenue). They went to live in a large house they called "Hopedene" on the Gorge waterfront, a couple of blocks west of Harriet. It was a substantial home, perfect for parties and dancing, with beautiful gardens terracing down

David M. Eberts

to the water—wonderful for regatta-watching.

Eberts' political career began in 1890 with his election to the provincial legislature. With only one interruption, he served as a member for Saanich for almost twenty years. In 1895 he was appointed attorney general, and he served in that office under three premiers—John Turner, James Dunsmuir, and E.G. Prior.

As politicians go, Eberts was more laid-back than most. Though he was a strong and eloquent speaker, he preferred to stay silent for the most part. But he was expert at handling hecklers, and if the occasion arose he was able to stand and address a particular question for more than twenty minutes at a time. "His words," declared the *Colonist,* "come in torrents and the members are taken by storm."

By the time the B.C. Electric Interurban line up the Saanich Peninsula was proposed, Eberts had been Speaker of the House under Premier Richard McBride for some years. Both Eberts and McBride were enthusiastic supporters of the interurban, and when the route was finally

David Eberts and Mabel Charles's 1884 wedding at Christ Church was followed by a reception at a Rockland Avenue home. The couple lived at "Hopedene," on the Gorge waterway.

established, a station was named in Eberts' honour as a supporter and as a much-respected local politician. In 1919 he was appointed to the bench, and remained a Supreme Court justice until he died, at age 74, in 1924.

That was the same year A.T. Goward proposed the underutilized, overexpensive Saanich line be shut down.

Albert Toller Goward was a Welshman, born in Tenby, South Wales, in 1874. After two years in insurance in Bristol and London, he moved to Victoria in 1890 at the age of eighteen and immediately joined the National Electric Tramway and Lighting Co. as a conductor. A

year later he was working in the office, and in 1897, when the B.C. Electric Railway Co. took over, he was appointed Victoria manager.

He was an efficient and popular manager. He was concerned enough about the welfare of his employees to foster a Sick and Death Benefit Association. Actuarial experts advised against providing sickness and death benefits, but Goward insisted and went on to guide the company through years of efficient operation.

Goward was also a keen sportsman. He won many trophies in men's singles, mixed, and men's doubles tennis competitions; was an enthusiastic soccer player, who captained the Victoria

Albert Toller Goward

A. T. Goward residence at York Place in Oak Bay.

Wanderers to the B.C. championship; captained the Victoria rugby team, which won provincial honours; was a cricketer of note; and later in life enjoyed a good game of golf.

When the company's Saanich line came into being, Goward had been BCER manager for fifteen years. It was Goward who carefully masterminded the line's opening and operation, and who proudly steadied the silver spike that Premier McBride hammered into the ground at Deep Bay.

A year after the Saanich line opened, it became clear that it wasn't paying its way—and it was facing competition from an unexpected source. As World War I gathered momentum in Europe, work was scarce and men looked for other ways to earn money. Some of them plied Victoria streets in small wheeled vehicles called jitneys (a jitney was a five-cent coin) or jalopies, picking people up and dropping them off wherever they wanted to go. The BCER slashed fares. Jitney operators protested. By the end of 1915, the BCER still wasn't holding its own.

The line struggled on for several more years, but in 1924, faced with rising costs and falling revenues, Goward finally recommended to the Minister of Railways that the Saanich line be discontinued. There were howls of protest, but the manager was right, and the end was near. Noting that the railway had promoted settlement in the Marigold, Glyn, and Eberts areas, the *Victoria Times* called the closure "the passing of an institution."

BCER officials posed for this photograph to commemorate the June 18, 1913 opening of Victoria's Interurban line. A.T. Goward is fourth from the left.

Eventually promoted to the position of BCER vice president, Goward retired in September 1945, after 50 years with the company. Less than a year later he died—like D.M. Eberts, at the age of 74—at his York Place home.

The station named in his honour was located where Goward Road is today, at the north end of what is now Interurban where it meets West Saanich Road. Eberts Station was above Wilkinson Station on Wilkinson Road, though the street named in his honour is off Dallas Road in the Ross Bay area.

STEVENS ROAD

A halt for the thirsty

*B*etween the Eberts and Goward stops, the railway rolled through Westwoodvale Station. "Westwood Farm" was the name given to the large house built on the former site of John Stevens' hotel.

Stevens was an Englishman, born in Gillingham, Kent, in 1835. As a boy, he went to sea with his uncle and spent time sailing up and down Canada's West Coast. His father's death took him home to England, but when his mother remarried—to a man Stevens didn't get along with—he left England once more, rejoined his uncle, and sailed back to the new colony across the sea.

It was fifteen years since the establishment of Fort Victoria. James Douglas, governor of the colony, ruled with an iron fist, and never more firmly than when the rush of miners to the gold fields of the Cariboo threatened to disrupt his empire. Suddenly a reasonably peaceful life in the settlement had been rudely disturbed. The population had doubled, quadrupled, swelled by the influx of men who cared nothing for the governor and his high-handed ways. They didn't stay long, but their presence was not a particularly positive force, and to make matters worse, they taught the local Natives bad habits, including a disregard for the law and a love of liquor.

When Douglas clamped down on the sale of liquor to Natives, Stevens' uncle was enraged. This had been a big part of his business. Stevens himself, less than thrilled with this latest turn of events and seeing no future for himself at sea, decided to start a new life on dry land. Where to live? Not near Douglas and his domain, that was for sure. He bought land out in the countryside, where the governor would be less likely to bother him.

The first pioneers had preceded him to the area called Saanich many years earlier. He travelled north on the trail they blazed, and when it forked, he veered left along the West Road and bought land for a farm. It was a good choice, especially when he decided to open a hotel. The trail was well used by people headed north. And at this point, there wasn't a watering hole in sight.

Stevens' tavern, built on a bend in the trail in full view of approaching traffic, quickly became known as a hospitable stop on the rough, uncomfortable journey up the peninsula. It was one mile past Royal Oak, six miles away from Victoria. In fact, it was roughly halfway between the town and Tod Inlet, so Stevens called it "Halfway House."

It's said that Stevens' wife, Georgina, prompted the family's move to another home.

John Stevens' Halfway House hostelry, built in 1861, stood almost opposite today's Beaver Lake Road, ready to provide a warm welcome to weary travellers heading up the peninsula.

Stevens' second hotel (pictured here in the 1890s) operated from the same site as its predecessor, on a sharp left-hand bend in West Saanich Road.

The futuristic structure of the Dominion Observatory (during construction in 1914) was a spectacular sight for Interurban passengers as they travelled north on the BCER line.

Stevens was a widower with a young daughter when he met and married Georgina. She was a native of Surrey, England, a widow with a young son, David. Two more daughters were born, and this may be what prompted Georgina to declare that a hotel was no place to bring up young children. They moved to a house on the western portion of Stevens' land. Stevens retired and handed over the hotel to his adopted son David. In 1907, 30 years after Governor Douglas's death, Stevens moved back to Victoria and bought a house at 27 South Turner Street in James Bay.

Little more than a decade later, the BC Electric Railway Interurban line extended north of Burnside with only one or two gentle curves along the way, then gently veered to the left, parallelling West Saanich Road and sweeping past a magnificent edifice high on a hill: the Dominion Observatory.

The new observatory was Victoria's pride and joy. Its telescope was the world's largest. On Saturdays, special trains took visitors to

Horsepower transported the world's largest telescope safely to its new home atop Observatory Hill.

fascinating lectures and demonstrations held there. Railway passengers alighting at Observatory Station had only to follow the signpost along a short footpath. At the end was the road leading to the summit. Spectacular sea and mountain views greeted the walkers at every turn on the winding ascent. Thanks to the Interurban line, the observatory was only 25 minutes away from downtown Victoria.

On its way to the observatory, the train stopped at Goward Station, not far from a large house with distinctive gables up on the hill to the left. This was the home John Stevens built for Georgina and their daughters. By the time the first railway car rolled past the house in 1913, Stevens was not long for this world. He died the next year while on a trip to California. He was buried at Ross Bay Cemetery and was joined there in 1929 by Georgina.

Like John Stevens, the railway is long gone. But just west of where Interurban runs into Goward, Stevens Road reminds us of the enterprising fellow from England who welcomed weary travellers at the Halfway House Hotel.

The BCER right-of-way near Westwoodvale, just south of Prospect Lake, stretched through undeveloped land.

PROSPECT LAKE ROAD

No gold in this glittering lake

On the Interurban line—unlike the V&S Railway—stops were frequent. Just a short distance north of Observatory Station, the train stopped again, this time at Prospect. From here it was an easy walk west to the lake with its waters glistening in the sunlight. North, south, and east lay lush farmland and family homes. By 1913, when crews cleared a track for the BC Electric Railway, they were working in the midst of a seasonal community that had been established many decades before by hunters, fishermen, and a few farmers.

It's said that Prospect Lake was so named, way back in the early days, because it was rumoured to contain gold. None was ever found, but the lake contained treasure of a different sort. Anglers were drawn to it like moths to a flame, especially after an item in the *Colonist* reported that one day in May 1867, six fishermen had caught 180 trout. Prospect Lake was a hunter's and fisher's paradise, and in the 1890s, when the V&S Railway made access easier, summer homes sprouted up on its shores. However, by the time the Duvals of Royal Oak—Louis and his son Fred—established their sawmill at the end of Sawmill Road (today's Meadowbrook Road) in 1907, there were still few permanent residents in the area.

The Duvals added their names to a petition asking the City of Victoria to build a road through from West Saanich Road to Prospect Lake. The City responded positively to the request, and Prospect Lake Road was completed shortly after. One of the foremen on the project was Sam McCullough, who later owned a general store and post office on West Saanich, opposite Prospect Lake Road. The store, which opened in 1913, was run by his daughter and son-in-law, Sadie and Jock Findlay. It served local residents and Interurban travellers, as well as those going north on the old West Road.

Horace and Edith Oldfield were early permanent settlers on Prospect Lake Road. Horace had bought property in Saanich soon after his arrival from England in 1895 and established a poultry and fruit farm. Each week he took his produce along the rough trail to Victoria. When he married Edith in 1910, he built a house on the property (now 260 Prospect Lake Road).

Before long, another branch of the family was living a short distance north, across West Saanich Road. John Henry Oldfield, Horace's cousin, was a native of Norfolk, England, who retired to Saanich with his wife Emma a year or two before the Interurban railway service began.

The Prospect Lake General Store, built in 1913 on the northwest side of the Sparton-West Saanich Road intersection opposite Prospect Lake Road, was a boon to local residents. The BCER offered easier access to Prospect Lake than the V&S, which left passengers facing a one-and-a-half mile hike from Beaver Lake.

He had bought 300 acres in 1903. His son Clarence and a friend cleared land for a house ready for his parents' arrival. Oldfield Senior called his large, Maclure-designed home "Norfolk Lodge," after his birthplace. It stands to this day at 5789 Brookhill Road. Clarence and his wife Doris built a home close by, then moved into his parents' home when John and Emma died. Oldfield Road perpetuates the family name.

Until Prospect Lake Road was completed, the only access to the lake was along rough trails. The V&S Railway carried visitors as far as Beaver Lake. From there, they could hike one and a half miles to Prospect Lake. If their homes were on the west side of the lake, people had to walk around or find someone to ferry them across.

Much of the land surrounding the lake belonged to a Chinese man by the name of On Hing. Like many of the early Chinese settlers, On Hing arrived in Victoria during the 1858 gold rush. He was hard-working and tireless, farming most of the 89 acres he owned around Prospect Lake and trading his produce and chickens all over the countryside. When On Hing died, his sons subdivided and sold his property and moved to Victoria. It was at this point—1914, one year after the Interurban service began—that Prospect Lake became a popular summer resort.

No more bone-bruising, best-part-of-a-day, horse-and-buggy rides along dirt roads for visitors from Victoria. The V&S had paved the way. Now the BC Electric provided an efficient, comfortable, half-hour ride from the city, dropping riders off at Goward or Prospect, within easy walking distance of the lake.

By the early 1920s, motor cars were within the reach of more than just the privileged few, but there was still no proper access to Prospect Lake from the south. In January 1922, local residents petitioned the Saanich Municipality for improvements to Prospect Lake Road, "the present condition of the road being a menace to the safety of people and property."

Presumably their request fell on deaf ears because eighteen months later they petitioned again. The residents made no bones about their feelings. "The road was never a good one," they declared, "but was made much worse since your honourable body cut down the timber thereon and turned same into cordwood, the hauling out of which at the time of year it was done badly cutting the same up and rendering it almost impossible for automobile traffic."

Eventually, the road was paved, thanks to the persistence of residents including the Oldfields and Frank Campbell. Frank was the son of Frank Campbell Sr., whose news and tobacco store, Campbell's Corner, had been a fixture on Government and Yates in the late

In the second decade of the 1900s, West Saanich Road was still a quiet, leafy route from Royal Oak to Deep Bay. The Interurban track, flanked by tall trees, ran close to a road that rarely saw an automobile.

1800s. Frank Jr. owned several acres on the west side of the lake.

By the time the road was finally paved, the Interurban line, which had been so important to the growth of the area, was closed. But the community remained.

SLUGGETT AVENUE

Brentwood began with the Sluggetts

Once past Prospect Lake, the Interurban line continued to parallel West Saanich Road, even joining it for a while as it ran north alongside Tod Creek. Then, rather than climb the long, steep hill that lay ahead, the line swung lazily left along what is now Wallace Drive. Walking or driving along this road today it's easy to imagine how it looked in the second decade of the twentieth century as the B.C. Electric Railway glided along its country track. And it's fascinating to follow its journey through the land and lives of the area's earliest pioneers.

Next stop on the line was Heals, at the western end of John Heal's acreage. In the 1860s Heal bought 50 acres that covered the area between the East Road (where the Pat Bay Highway is today) and the West Road and stretched as far north as Durrance. Two of his sons later bought more land. When Charles Heal's West Saanich Road property was sold, it became a rifle range— the next stop on the Interurban line. Then it was on to Durrance.

John Durrance

John Durrance had arrived in Victoria from Leicestershire, England, via California, in 1860. He settled in Saanich on a large acreage along what became Durrance Road and, like many early settlers, painstakingly cleared his own land using teams of oxen. In 1871 he married Jane Cheeseman Bailey of Royal Oak, who had been widowed for the second time a few months earlier. Jane and her five children moved to Durrance's Spring Valley Farm.

The next year a son, John Durrance Jr., was born there. He grew up, married, and built a home (now 155 Durrance) just west of his parents' farmhouse. By the time the Interurban track was laid along the eastern part of Spring Valley Farm, John Sr. was gone, but a succession of John Durrances continued to keep the family name alive.

Beyond Durrance, the next stop on the line was Tod Inlet, where a spur line ran down through the Greig property to Robert Pym Butchart's British Columbia Cement Plant. The road from the plant, named Benvenuto after the Butcharts' home, crossed Wallace and continued

In 1913, members of the Durrance family wait at the Durrance Station for the arrival of the Interurban. The B.C. Electric's Interurban ran through farmland near Durrance Station, on what is now Wallace Drive (inset).

to run east till it reached West Saanich Road. In those early days after the Butcharts' 1904 arrival, Tod Inlet was a small, somewhat isolated village. The Interurban line provided a welcome link with civilization.

Not far north of Tod Inlet was Sluggetts Station, named for the family that at one point owned much of the land in the area.

Born in Thornbury, Devonshire, John Sluggett, a carpenter by trade, brought his bride to Canada three weeks after their wedding. The voyage from Plymouth to Quebec was tempestuous and terrifying—an eleven-week nightmare that drove Fanny to declare that she could never attempt it again. For twenty years Sluggett farmed in various Ontario villages before bringing his wife and their seven children out to B.C. in the 1870s.

Sluggett bought land that once belonged to a Hudson's Bay Company man—an acreage on the Saanich Peninsula that covered the area from the shores of the inlet to East Saanich Road. He moved his family into an abandoned fourteen-by-twenty-foot log cabin on the trail that later

Fanny Sluggett

for, and built, the area's first place of worship—Sluggett Memorial Baptist Church—in his honour. They continued to farm the land they had inherited, and even after the Interurban line made fast transport of milk and produce possible, they still drove wagonloads down the West Saanich Road to Victoria each week.

It was also in 1909 that the village of Sluggetts was renamed Brentwood Bay by R.M. Horne-Payne, late of Brentwood, Essex, England, and president of the B.C. Electric Railway Co. from 1897 to 1928. In 1975, 100 years after John Sluggett's arrival here, his

became Benvenuto, then built them a larger home near the intersection of today's West Saanich Road and Sluggett Avenue.

There was much work to be done to clear the land and build barns, and the Sluggetts' many years of farming experience stood them in good stead. It didn't take them long to become self-sufficient, always well supplied with meat, poultry, butter, eggs, and Fanny Sluggett's specialty—Devonshire cream.

Concerned about his children's education, Sluggett donated land for a school close by. He also ran a post office from his farm, one of three (the others were at Hagan's and Heal's) that supplied mail service to the area.

Eventually Sluggett owned more than 1,100 acres. When he died in 1909, his property was divided among his seven children. He had been instrumental in starting a Sunday school for the local children, so the Sluggett boys donated land

Heal's was one of several post offices along the route that handled the peninsula's mail. Before there were post offices, mail was often delivered to and picked up from the area's hotels.

In the 1930s, a look north along West Saanich Road and its intersection with Wallace Drive reveals that horsepower was still more prevalent than gas-power. Hayracks like Lorne Thomson's were a familiar sight. Centre left, beside the top of the hayrack, is the old West Saanich School (now a Scout Hall), and on the corner an automobile stands near a gas pump outside the food store (now a supermarket).

descendants—including all seven branches of the family—gathered to reminisce and remember the couple whose name lives on in the community of Brentwood Bay.

Today Brentwood's streets bristle with many other pioneer names: Marchant, Hagan, Peden, and Verdier. At the foot of Verdier Avenue—originally the skid road that the Verdiers ran their logs down—is a building that houses the Moodyville General Store. Who, we may wonder, was Mr. Moody?

In the latter part of the 1800s, B.C. became home to two well-known men by the name of Moody. The first, and best known, was Richard Clement Moody, a colonel in the Royal Engineers, who arrived in Victoria in 1858 with his wife, four children, and a team of engineers to help Governor James Douglas choose a site

for B.C.'s new capital. Douglas favoured Fort Langley; Moody persuaded him that the New Westminster riverfront was farther from the American border and better suited for residential and commercial development. In 1863, when the Royal Engineers were disbanded, the Moodys returned to England. Port Moody, the original western terminus of the Canadian Pacific Railway, reminds us of the colonel's presence here.

The Moody of Saanich Inlet fame was the American who had established a sawmill at Moodyville (now called North Vancouver) on the north shore of Burrard Inlet. Sewell Prescott Moody eventually moved to Saanich, lending his name to the general store and today's Moody Crescent.

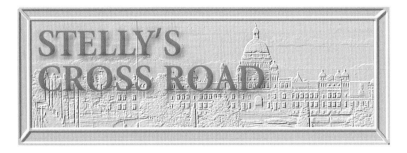

STELLY'S CROSS ROAD

Water brought him wealth

*L*eaving the bustle of Brentwood behind, the Interurban railway followed Wallace Drive through Sluggett land and over what was fondly known as "the flats" on its way to Stelly's. If the track had continued its course due east, it would have crossed the V&S Railway line (today's Veyaness Road). Then it would have rolled right through the churchyard at Shady Creek, where John and Fanny Sluggett lie buried.

Fortunately for Saanich Baptist Church, as Shady Creek was once called, the Interurban line was headed north. Near where the old spur line ran off at Willow, the track eased gently around a long, lazy bend—a smooth sweep through still-peaceful countryside to the station at Stelly's Cross Road.

George Stelly was a native of Switzerland, born there in 1825. In 1851 he journeyed west to seek his fortune. From Liverpool, on England's north-west coast, he set sail for America. The ship carried him to New Orleans and on up the Mississippi to St. Louis. Stelly's first job in the New World—he was a ploughman—paid him enough to move on into Iowa. He joined others bound for the West Coast. There was safety in numbers. Crossing the country in a covered wagon, through Indian territory, they guarded themselves day and night against attack.

The hoped-for fortune didn't materialize in California, but Stelly earned enough to enable him to move north to seek gold on the Fraser River. Like other early prospectors, he came first to Vancouver Island, sailing into Esquimalt one June day in 1858 and walking east along the rough three-mile trail to the settlement on Victoria's harbour.

Soon he was on his way to the mainland, but success eluded him again. By the spring of 1859 he was back, broke but far from broken. He set to work as a labourer and before long was able to buy a

George and Katherine Stelly

mule and cart for his latest money-making venture—selling water to local residents. In those far-off days before a steady supply was piped in from Elk Lake, water was brought down from Spring Ridge. At 25 cents a bucket, Stelly's simple house-to-house delivery system soon put him on the road to financial freedom.

He married a German girl called Katherine and continued to prosper. By the time their son George reached school age, they could afford to send him to Switzerland to be educated. Unfortunately, young George had an accident there in which he suffered a severe spinal injury.

When he was brought back to Victoria, his father decided to buy 200 acres of farmland in Saanich.

The farm extended from the shores of Saanich Inlet, through the area called Moodyville, to East Saanich Road. The Stellys

Descendants of the first generation of Butlers, shown outside their country home at Keating, retain property in the area to this day. Inset is of George and Fanny Butler.

By 1905 some locals were getting around in a new invention, the automobile, but the condition of the roads, like this one near Mount Newton and West Saanich, made every outing an adventure.

divided their time between their downtown home and their farm. Katherine died in 1890, and in 1913, the year the Interurban started to run through George Stelly's land and stop at Stellys Station, he too was laid to rest.

Onward and upward ran the line, creeping ever closer to its competitor, the V&S. At Saanichton the two lines actually ran parallel, and both had a stop. Here, in the heart of Saanich, you had a choice—you could transfer to the Sidney line and spend some time at the Prairie Inn or dance the night away at the Agricultural Fair.

Saanichton, lying almost halfway between the peninsula's east and west shores, had long been its social centre. Starting in the 1850s, early pioneers including the Thomsons, Turgooses, Lidgates, Marcottes, Simpsons, and others had

formed a tight-knit community. They built a church—St. Stephens—and a school along what is now Mt. Newton Cross Road.

The first teacher at the school was a young Englishwoman by the name of Mrs. Butler. George and Fanny Butler, both from Hampshire, England, had married in Victoria in 1868 and arrived in Saanich soon after. Captain Butler was an infantryman who had served in the Crimea and at the Battle of Sebastopol before being posted to Quebec. Hearing of the gold find on the Fraser River, he had tried his luck there, with modest success, and had eventually decided to settle in Saanich. He took a keen interest in local matters and became first secretary of the Saanich Agricultural Fair.

As far as the community was concerned, the Butlers were both welcome…but Fanny was nothing less than a godsend. Trained as a governess in England, she was the perfect person to teach at the local school. She was also an accomplished pianist. She even had her own piano, sent around the Horn by her father as a wedding gift. Always willing to share her considerable talents, she allowed her precious piano to be carted from one social event to another, and somehow managed to get a decent tune out of it when it reached its destination.

George Butler bought land along Keating Cross Road. He died in 1885, but Fanny was still alive when the Interurban trains started to run north across Keating and Stelly's to Saanichton. She died in 1920, but miraculously, her piano survived. Lovingly restored, it now resides at the Saanich Pioneers Society's Log Cabin for all to see—a reminder of the days when a social occasion wasn't complete without music provided by the captain's talented wife.

TATLOW ROAD

"Minister of fruit and finances"

Continuing along Wallace Drive from its Saanichton stop, the Interurban train swung east, running parallel with the V&S line through land first farmed by pioneers with names such as John, Harrison, and Sadler. Rolling on toward Sidney, the B.C. Electric line ran through today's Experimental Farm, then along what is now Mainwaring Road and across Breed's Cross Road (now McTavish), over land owned by families whose names live on on the peninsula today—the Sandovers, Reays, McIlmoyles, Imries, and more.

There were stops at Bazan Bay, Tripp, and Sidneway. Because of a previous agreement with the V&S, this was the closest the BCER was allowed to come to the village of Sidney, so the track swerved west, then ran north again right through the middle of what is now the Victoria International Airport. It crossed George Mills' and Henry Wain's roads, turned at Horth Hill, and headed west toward Deep Bay. The track passed through land that once belonged to Lowen and Erb, along today's Tatlow Road. Unlike other roads in the area, this was not named after a pioneer farmer, but a politician.

Robert Garnet Tatlow was an Irishman, born in Co. Down in 1855. He arrived in Montreal in 1877 and joined the Royal Canadian Artillery. Two years later he was posted to Victoria as part of "B" battery, quartered in Beacon Hill Park. A year later he left the army and sent for Miss May Leaycraft, the young lady who had been waiting for him in Quebec. They met and married in San Francisco.

Robert Tatlow

Tatlow brought his new bride back to Victoria, where he was private secretary to Lieutenant Governor A.N. Richards, and then to his successor, Clement Francis Cornwall.

In 1886 Captain Tatlow resigned his post at Government House and took his wife and daughter Mabel to Vancouver, where he joined a group investing in real estate. Then tragedy struck. On Christmas Eve of that year, 25-year-old May died in childbirth. Mother and stillborn second

*Helen and Margaret, the daughters of
Tatlow's second marriage, to Susan Cambie.*

*Robert Tatlow and his
daughter Helen in 1909.*

daughter were laid to rest together in Victoria. It
was seven years before Tatlow married again, this
time to the daughter of H.J. Cambie, chief
engineer of the Canadian Pacific Railway's
Pacific division.

Tatlow immersed himself in politics. Twice
defeated for the legislature, he won a seat in
1900, and in 1903 Premier Richard McBride
appointed him Minister of Finance and
Agriculture. Back in Victoria once more, "Fruit
and Finances" Tatlow installed his family in a
big house called "Maple Croft," on Dallas Road,
before moving them to Pemberton Road and,
eventually, Rockland. In 1908 his oldest

daughter, Mabel, was married to Fitzalan
Cornwall, son of Tatlow's former employer.

Tatlow loved horses. Even when automobiles
became more popular, he insisted on driving his
own pony and trap. One day in April 1910, an
attempt to avert disaster cost him his life. Trying
to stop a runaway horse and carriage at the
corner of Vancouver and McClure streets, he
fell under the wheels. He later died of the severe
injuries sustained in that accident.

When the B.C. Electric Railway's Saanich line
opened three years later, Premier Richard
McBride remembered his respected former
colleague. He drove the last spike in the line at

Deep Bay, at the end of the track that ran through Tatlow Station on what is now Tatlow Road.

Tatlow had been gone six years when the "Big Snow" came in 1916. Intermittent snowfall through January culminated in a major dump on February 3, when Victoria found itself under four feet of snow that had been whipped by winds into ten-foot high drifts. Soldiers trained for war fought a battle with the elements, clearing city streets so that people in outlying areas could be supplied with food, fuel and other necessities. The Saanich line, its locomotive equipped with a snowplough, kept right on rolling.

Despite its sterling efforts and steady reliability, the line still suffered financially. In a never-ending struggle to compete for business, passenger fares were lowered: Victoria to Sidney and return cost 50 cents. The V&S retaliated by lowering its fares too. The BCER rallied with expansion and improvements to the Chalet near the line's Deep Bay (now Deep Cove) terminus.

When Tatlow returned to Victoria with his second wife, Susan Cambie Tatlow (inset), and their daughters, he first moved into a big house on Dallas Road, "Maple Croft," before settling in Rockland.

Three men whose names are connected with the B.C. Electric Railway's Interurban line appear in the front row of this photo of the B.C. legislative assembly in 1908: Richard McBride (second from left), David Eberts (centre), and Robert Tatlow (second from right).

The two lines struggled side by side for another few years. The V&S succumbed first, in 1919. By 1924, B.C. Electric's Saanich line was also defunct. One of its chief competitors was the automobile, more prolific since the 1917 surge in road surfacing and paving. The other was yet another railway line on the peninsula, with a terminus just a short distance south of BCER's own.

No need to get stranded at Deep Cove. All we have to do is go down to Patricia Bay and catch the Canadian Northern Railway back to Victoria!

CANORA ROAD

The last peninsula railway

I t's hard to believe that in the second decade of the 1900s, when the whole of Vancouver Island north of Victoria had only one major railroad—the Esquimalt & Nanaimo (E&N) line—the 32-kilometre-long Saanich Peninsula had no less than three. Transportation had come a long way from its humble beginnings more than half a century before.

In the 1850s the first settlers who moved north of Fort Victoria travelled on foot or on horseback along rough trails. Land was cleared for farming by teams of oxen. Horses and wagons, still a luxury for many, were much prized. Decades later, the advent of "motors," as automobiles were called, caused the peninsula's trails to be turned into rough, unpaved country roads, full of potholes and craters that became miniature lakes after a rainfall. By the 1890s travel was still hazardous and painfully slow, so people in outlying areas north of the now-bustling city of Victoria greeted the news of a railway line with glee.

The V&S Railway opened for business in 1894, connecting Victoria with Sidney and promising a sea link with the Island's east coast and the mainland. The mainland connection, which faced stiff competition from the Canadian Pacific fleet, was a disappointment, and in 1913,

when the B.C. Electric Company's Interurban line offered a faster and more satisfactory sea link from its terminus at Deep Bay, Victorians speedily transferred their allegiance. But the Interurban was itself outsmarted by the inauguration, in 1917, of the Canadian Northern Pacific Railway line connecting Victoria with Patricia Bay.

It was a long time before the first spike was driven for the Vancouver Island section of the CNPR. Construction on the Victoria-Port Alberni line started just beyond Four Mile House in 1911. The idea was to compete with the Canadian Pacific Railroad for the silk market of the Orient. Ships from Asia would land at Victoria and the valuable cargo would connect to the CNPR line into the Fraser Valley, thus bypassing Vancouver. Progress was slow, until the advent of World War I in 1914 changed the focus from silk to Sitka spruce. Anxious to help the war effort, the federal government chipped in funds for the railway's completion, but it was too late. By the time the CNPR's up-Island line was ready for service, the war was over. Seven years later the line had connected Victoria with Lake Cowichan, Youbou, and Nitinat, but the economic slump of the late 1920s put an end to plans for Port Alberni.

The railway line made Patricia Bay more accessible to city dwellers. Picnics, games, and races along the beach were favourite summer pastimes.

The Saanich Peninsula section fared better. Construction began in 1912 on a line that was to pass up the east side of the peninsula, crossing over to the west side below Sidney, and ending at Patricia Bay. A long trestle built out over the mudflats provided access to seagoing transport for passengers and freight heading to the mainland docks at Port Mann.

At the other end of the line, another long trestle was required to cross the Gorge at Selkirk Water. While it was being constructed, a temporary southern terminus was built at Alpha Street, on the northern edge of the city, but before the line could be completed, war broke out, bringing with it a shortage of rail. Construction ground to a halt until 1916.

The Saanich service eventually started in April 1917. Compared to the hoopla that surrounded the opening of the V&S and Interurban lines, inauguration of CNPR passenger service received relatively little fuss. Officials had great hopes for the line, which opened up parts of the peninsula that had not been served by rail before. A surge in growth was anticipated, particularly down the east side, which had remained relatively unpopulated. There was an explosives factory on James Island, and workers who previously faced a long hike into Sidney to pick up the V&S now had more accessible transportation. Nearer to Victoria, the arrival of the CNPR meant the narrow strip of land east of Elk Lake could be developed into something more than a summer picnic and vacation spot.

Success seemed assured, but it wasn't to be. As cars and buses became more popular and the

In 1904, an automobile ride along West Saanich Road to Patricia Bay was a treat for people who lived in the town. In those days, Native homes lined the road south of the beach.

roads they ran along were improved, all three railway lines found themselves in fierce competition for a dwindling amount of business. The V&S was first to bite the dust, going into receivership in 1919.

By this time, Canadian National had taken over Canadian Northern Pacific. When the V&S closed, CNR paid out more than $25,000 for the Pat Bay-Sidney connecting line so that freight and lumber could still be transported by rail directly to Victoria.

In 1924, B.C. Electric closed its Interurban line. Canadian National reigned supreme in Saanich—for one more decade. The company closed its peninsula line to passengers in October 1924, and in 1927, construction of a new barge

slip at Point Ellice meant that freight from Lake Cowichan no longer had to be transported up to Patricia Bay for shipment off-Island. This greatly reduced traffic on the line, and a few years later, when the Sidney mill closed and a storm caused extensive damage to the northern terminus's barge slip, its fate was sealed. By 1935, 40 years after the Cordwood Express had first huffed and puffed up the peninsula and 20 years after the first Interurban train drove smoothly up to Deep Bay, the once-promising rail link between Victoria and North Saanich was gone for good.

Today, walkers and cyclists follow the old Canora line's right of way along the Galloping Goose Trail.

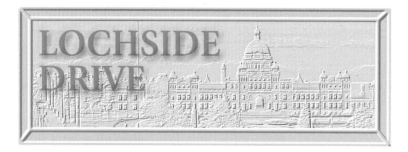

LOCHSIDE DRIVE

Ticket to summer fun

*A*t the northern end of the Canora line, the CNPR trestle pointed its 670-metre-long wooden finger out from the shore, across the mudflats, and into the deep waters of what was once called Union Bay. The sweeping curve of water, with its perfect-for-picnics sandy beach, had been renamed for the pretty young princess who visited Victoria with her father, the Duke of Connaught, in 1912.

A few years later, young boys who dreamed of becoming train engineers watched with fascination as huge barges carrying loaded railway cars tied up at the end of the trestle. Soon the steamship *Canora* (named, like Canora Road, for the CAnadian NOrthern RAilway) joined the service, bringing freight and passengers from the CNPR's mainland terminal at Port Mann.

The railway cars edged carefully across the mudflats to the shore at the south end of the bay. Just north of the

Union Bay was renamed Patricia Bay in honour of Princess Patricia, who visited Victoria in 1912.

terminus, behind a protective cluster of trees, stood Holy Trinity Church, with its distinctive lych-gate and wooden-fenced churchyard. The track ran southeast from the waterfront, approximately following today's Willingdon Road, through property once farmed by pioneers such as George Mills and the Reay brothers.

Where McTavish Road meets today's Pat Bay Highway, the three peninsula railway lines almost touched. The Canora crossed the B.C. Electric track, then the V&S track, as it made for the shoreline at Bazan Bay. On rolled the train, through land once owned by the Sandovers, Sadlers, Johns, and Turgooses.

In 1912, the B.C. Electric Railway purchased just under 50 hectares of Edmund Sadler's heavily timbered land west of the Canora track. Today this property is home to the Dominion Experimental Farm, a plant quarantine

This view east over the Experimental Farm toward Cordova Channel in earlier, pre-Pat Bay Highway days, shows the B.C. Electric Interurban and CNPR's Canora lines running left to right across the landscape.

station where farm research scientists ensure that fruit and other plants coming into Canada from foreign countries are free of viruses.

Leaving the shoreline to continue almost due south, the train headed for Michell Station, located at what is now Lochside and Island View. Like several other early Saanich pioneers, Thomas Michell was a Welshman. He and his wife Margaret came to this area in late 1862. Michell twice tried his luck in the Cariboo gold fields, making enough money to open a grocery and confectionery store downtown and, eventually, to move his family out to Saanich. After more than 40 years of farm life, the Michells retired and moved back to Victoria. By the time the Canora rolled through their land in 1917, both Thomas and Margaret had died, but their descendants ensure that the farm and the family name live on to this day.

Michell Station was the last stop before a seaside spot that was the highlight of the trip for most Canora passengers—Cordova Bay.

It was Manuel Quimper, a sub-lieutenant in the Spanish navy, who in 1790 named these waters after Don Antonio Maria Bucareli y Ursua Henestrosa Lasso de la Vega Villacis y Cordova. Apart from having one of the longest names in the world, Cordova was also 46th Viceroy of New Spain. Quimper gave his name to the channel that separated Bazan Bay from James Island, and to the harbour at Esquimalt. Hudson's Bay Company officials later restored the latter's First Nations name, and declared that the sweeping beach between Cowichan Head and Cormorant Point on the east side of the peninsula was to be known as Cordova Bay.

Long before the HBC and the Spaniards came on the scene, Cordova Bay belonged to people of the Songhees Nation. In winter they stayed close to their camp, up on the bank above the beach. In summer they built and repaired boats and travelled on foot and by canoe, gathering food and supplies for the long dark months ahead. In October, potlatches provided an opportunity for sharing and communication

Originally from Swansea, in Wales, Thomas and Margaret Michell arrived in Victoria in 1862. Thomas mined gold on the mainland with more than moderate success, bought land on the Saanich Peninsula, and moved his family out to it in March 1868. The Michells became well-respected members of the farming community. Margaret died in 1912 and Thomas died in 1916, one year before the CNPR's peninsula line opened for service.

between villages. Then it was winter, and the cycle began again.

Had their numbers not been decimated by disease and the damage done by firearms, and had their land not been appropriated by the HBC, the Songhees would probably be there still. But by 1919, when the Canora's locomotive nosed its way into the station on the southeast corner of Haliburton and Lochside, those simple early days were long gone. On the same beach where the Songhees once held clambakes, white people now had picnics. Families with names like Touet, Norris, Carmichael, Jeune, and Johns owned property along the waterfront. Cordova Bay had turned into a thriving community, a place where city dwellers weary of Victoria's hustle and bustle could spend lazy summers by the sea.

Many of the area's first permanent settlers were summer folk who decided to stay. Father

might continue to work in the city, travelling home on weekends along the winding, heavily forested road from Cedar Hill by horse and buggy, by jitney, or—once the Canora was up and running—by train.

In an area that seemed designed for swimming, hiking, and fishing, there was no shortage of things to do. Children played on the safe sandy beach from dawn to dusk, and gathered around bonfires after dark. Ice creams dripped deliciously down dimpled chins, while mothers relaxed with friends at the shoreside tearooms, where they could keep a watchful eye on their young ones.

It was an ideal, blissful existence. But for many of the visitors, summer was over all too soon and it was time to take the Canora back to town.

Cordova Bay was the scene of many a special event, like the 1886 Victoria Spiritualists Society picnic, pictured here. Many well-known Victoria citizens turned to spiritualism for one reason or another, including Mayor James Fell (in white waistcoat, standing at centre), who was still mourning the death of his wife Sarah, and photographer Hannah Maynard (seated at right, in profile), who turned to spiritualism after the death of her daughter Lillian.

Temporary terminus for the CNPR

The Canora left the south end of Cordova Bay over land that had been farmed since 1879 by Channel Islander Phillip Touet. He was the first man to settle permanently there, on property purchased from absentee landowner Samuel Haseltine. Touet's log cabin sat in solitary splendour amidst huge trees close to the shoreline near today's D'Arcy Lane.

A rough wagon road connected him with the Carmichael farm along the bay to the north. Indian trails led him west to R.P. Rithet's Broadmead estate at Royal Oak, or south to James Tod's farm, and thence to Victoria. In the 1890s the City of Victoria paid Touet to build a wagon road from the south end of the bay and round the east side of Mount Douglas. This gave Cordova Bay settlers more direct access to Victoria. Touet built it the "easy" way—skirting outcroppings of rock, avoiding the biggest trees—and created the pleasant, winding road that drivers follow to this day.

When the CNPR rolled through Cordova Bay, it ignored Touet's scenic route. Instead, the Canora track threaded its way through Rithet's place, crossed today's Royal Oak Drive, and continued south along the west side of what is now called the Blenkinsop Valley.

Cordova Bay residents had greeted the 1905 opening of Lost Lake (later Blenkinsop) Road with delight. Previously the journey to Victoria entailed a long, winding ride along the north and eastern edges of Mount Douglas, then down the length of Cedar Hill Road. No matter that Blenkinsop often flooded and the roadbed had to be matted with crisscrossed fir and cedar branches, then layered with gravel. For the most part, it provided easier horse-and-buggy access to town.

Flooding wasn't an issue for train travellers. The Canora's gas-powered cars sped along the track toward Lost (Blenkinsop) Lake, then crossed the lake at its midpoint, soaring over the surface on a long trestle before continuing south. Numerous springs fed the fertile farmland. Still lake waters, studded with beaver dams, provided a haven for fish, birds, and other wild creatures. Then, as now, signs along Blenkinsop Road warned that deer might cross your path.

In the early 1900s the valley was quiet and peaceful. On its eastern side, where the land sloped down from Cedar Hill (now Mount Douglas), property that once belonged to HBC trader George Blenkinsop had been subdivided and sold, to be enjoyed by families such as the Glendinnings and the Simmondses.

Phillip Touet was the first man to build a home at the south end of Cordova Bay.

Adam Glendinning was a Scotsman who came to this area in the 1870s and bought a large acreage in the valley. His property's eastern border stretched below Mount Douglas, while the western edge ran through the middle of Lost Lake. In those days the lake was almost a mile long and a third as wide—a fine place for a rowboat on a Sunday afternoon. Uncleared land surrounding the lake sported a variety of trees—cedar, fir, willow, alder, and birch—that were home to large numbers of wild pigeons. The bush and the trees were so thick that the lake could not be seen from afar; it was literally "lost" amongst them.

Early in the 1900s, Glendinning moved his family to the new home he had built for them higher up the slope, and he sold the western portion of his land. One of the purchasers was William Mercer, whose first home was on Alpha Street, where the CNPR's temporary terminus would later be built.

First one cow, then several, supplied the Mercers and their neighbours with milk. But William wanted a farm and a full-sized dairy, so when the Blenkinsop Valley opened up, he bought 125 acres of Glendinning property. Timber for the railway trestle that crossed the

In the days when such items were still a rarity, Frank Borden was justifiably proud of his 1912 Overland car.

lake came from Mercer's land. Through the 1900s, the remains of the trestle—a cluster of pilings formed from those long-ago trees—stretched out from the south shore of the lake.

Mercer expanded his property by 75 acres when his neighbours to the south, the Simmonds brothers, decided to sell. Harry, Monty, Arthur, and Tom Simmonds had been in B.C. since 1902, when Arthur bought land from Glendinning. Their sister Frances joined them some time later. They owned all the valley property from Mercer's down to North Dairy Farm. The railway track cut through their western boundary to Cedar Hill Cross Road and on into Borden's land.

Nova Scotian Frank Borden and his brother-in-law, Dudley Pickard, had signed the lease on the Hudson's Bay Company's North Dairy Farm in 1894. Their 300 acres were bounded by Blenkinsop to the east and Kenneth McKenzie's Lake Hill Farm to the west, and stretched south to what was originally Dr. W.F. Tolmie's Cloverdale Farm. Frank and Millie Borden, married in 1895, raised their family on the farm and established a business, Borden Mercantile, that thrives at Borden and McKenzie to this day.

After leaving Borden's property, the CNPR track curved behind today's Saanich Centre and veered across the marsh to Swan Lake. Another

*A trestle (pictured here in the early 1930s) carried the Canora
across Blenkinsop Lake at its mid-point. The trestle was recently
rebuilt and now forms part of the Galloping Goose Trail.*

*Another trestle carried the Canora track high above the southern edge of
Swan Lake, today the home of the Swan Lake Nature Sanctuary.*

Fred Borden was pictured in the 1930s in a field on North Dairy Farm. His brother
Frank signed the lease on the 300-acre farm, one of several in this area, in 1894.

trestle carried it along the southern edge of what is now a nature sanctuary. A steel bridge spanned North Douglas (now the Trans-Canada Highway), creating a junction that allowed cars to follow a new route west to Sooke and beyond. South of the junction, on Alpha Street near Burnside, the CNPR built a temporary terminus until it completed the trestle over Selkirk Water that would carry the train on to Victoria West. The area that lay between the Point Ellice (Bay Street) and Johnson Street bridges, studded with railway sheds and criss-crossed with railway lines, echoed to the rattle of steel-wheeled railcars, readying themselves for the journey back up to the junction and out to Sooke.

EDWARD MILNE ROAD

The Cowichan connection

North of the Alpha Street Station, the Canadian National Railway, as the old Canora was now called, turned west at the junction. This was supposed to be the beginning of a lucrative link between Victoria and Port Alberni. However, although construction of the up-Island section of the track had started in 1911, progress was painfully slow and there were many disappointments along the way.

For a start, the proposed route was somewhat circuitous, weaving its way through the Western Communities before turning north toward Cowichan. So far, so good. But establishing a right of way from east to west through the dense vegetation along the north shore of Cowichan Lake proved more difficult than expected. The forest's undergrowth and shrubs, force-fed by a constant drizzle of rain, were taller than the men who challenged them and posed a hazard to any who wandered off the beaten track.

Then the war years intervened. Efforts were renewed in late 1918, but the construction crews were fighting a losing battle. Parts of the track were already overgrown. Wooden bridges and trestles, deemed safe for only ten years, would have to be replaced soon after the line opened for business.

The Cowichan extension was completed in 1924. The line pushed beyond Youbou to

Edward Milne Jr. arrived in Sooke with wife Janet and his parents in 1883. Milne built a wharf to receive freight from Victoria, opened a general store and post office in 1893, and served as postmaster for more than 40 years.

In 1854, William Parson, a millwright at Millstream Sawmill, built a bridge with a hostelry on its north side six miles from Fort Victoria. Parson's Bridge Hotel was a welcome sight for travellers along the trail to Metchosin and sailors from Esquimalt Harbour. By the time the Galloping Goose glided along beside it, the original structure had been replaced by today's Six Mile House Hotel (pictured here at the turn of the century).

Kissinger (now Nitinat) by 1928, but never did make it as far as Port Alberni. Victorians didn't mind. They were happy to be able to travel as far as Sooke.

Passenger service didn't begin until late 1922, but for anyone who had ever endured a long, bumpy, stagecoach ride to the farming communities west of the city, it was well worth the wait. There was a whole new world to explore at the end of the meandering railway line, and lots of interesting whistle-stops along the way.

And it was a quick trip, too. The 30-passenger gas-powered car, nicknamed the Galloping Goose, made short work of the journey to and from Victoria.

The CN terminal was now located near the west end of the Point Ellice (Bay Street) Bridge, rebuilt since the 1896 streetcar disaster that took so many lives. From here, the one-car "train" ran past the Point Ellice station house (which stands at the west end of the bridge to this day) and on up to the North

This view east across the Sooke River, ca. 1910, shows the Milne home (highest building, left of centre) and the post office-general store. Edward Milne Jr. served as postmaster from 1895 to 1940. The station at Milnes Landing was the last stop before Leechtown on the CN line.

Douglas junction, near today's Town & Country shopping centre. Then it headed west, running along the north side of Portage Inlet and through land once owned by Dr. J.S. Helmcken. Just north of Price's Bay, the CN met the E&N and ducked under it. The two danced along side by side through the station behind Six Mile House, where William Parson had built the first hotel almost 50 years before. The track was smooth. There were trestles galore. It was an exhilarating ride.

Past Mill Hill, the two lines went their separate ways. The E&N headed for Langford, Goldstream, and points north. The CN rounded Colwood Corners and ducked south of what is now the Royal Colwood Golf Club, running along near the West Coast Highway (now Sooke Road) opposite James Dunsmuir's Hatley Park estate.

As though longing for some fun, the CN turned left at Luxton to head through Happy Valley. Running along west of where Thomas Blinkhorn built Bilston Farm in 1851, the line continued south through the close-knit community that had changed little since Blinkhorn's day. Houses dotted the landscape. Livestock looked on as the train rolled by. Farms and meadowland stretched in all directions along the valleys and up the lower mountain slopes.

The CN ran west of the community's main centre and crossed diagonally through the Rocky Point-Kangaroo Road intersection. Turning abruptly before Mary Hill, just west of Weir Beach, the track followed the north shore of Matheson Lake, rounded a bend at Roche Cove, and ran up the shoreline to meet Sooke Road. Hugging the shoreline for a while, it crossed Sooke Road and ran alongside it to Saseenos Station. This was the end of the line for many passengers, especially during the summer months when they came to picnic and swim on the sweeping curve of the beach.

From here, it was a hop, skip, and a jump to Edward Milne's place. Long before the railway arrived, the Milnes farmed in the area and ran a general store at the corner of Sooke and Sooke River roads. A wharf allowed boats that were carrying merchandise and materials to land close by. Years later, Milnes Landing Station became the last stop on the line before Leechtown, where in 1864 a survey team led by Lieutenant Peter Leech had found gold.

By the mid-1920s, CN was providing regular freight service to the many logging operations that had sprung up along the Cowichan section of the line, but few people regularly went past Leechtown. The CN passenger service, conceived in a gentler time and cursed by the advent of the automobile, lasted only a few more years. By 1932, the Galloping Goose was gone.

So ended—at least for the southern end of Vancouver Island—the remarkable era of rail travel. Transportation had come a long way since Captain W.C. Grant, first settler in Sooke, was forced to travel twenty miles up the coast by canoe in 1849 because there wasn't even a rough trail beyond Metchosin. Over the next 80 years, progress was slow but steady. Gold finds in the Cariboo and later the Klondike transformed the small Hudson's Bay Company settlement into a thriving commercial centre. Pioneer pathways became roads and railways. Sea travel changed too. Tall-masted sailing ships were replaced by paddle-wheeled steamers and eventually by huge ocean liners. Over the decades, navigators, sea captains, and sailors from near and far helped put Vancouver Island, and Victoria, on the map. Along the way they named points and places of interest around the coastline and even helped build some of those early pioneer pathways…

But that's a story for another book.

Although the service extended beyond it, Leechtown was the end of the line for most CN passengers. Pictured in 1926, this group watched and waited for the Galloping Goose to cruise around the curve on the approach to Leechtown Station.

BIBLIOGRAPHY

Source material at the British Columbia Archives and Records Service, City of Victoria Archives, Saanich Municipal Archives, Esquimalt Municipal Archives, Saanich Pioneer Society, Sooke Region Museum, and the Greater Victoria Public Library was supplemented with information gleaned while reading and enjoying the following books:

∞ ∞ ∞ ∞

Adams, John. *Historic Guide to Ross Bay Cemetery*. Victoria, BC: Sono Nis Press, 1998.

Akrigg, G.P.V. and Helen B. Akrigg. *British Columbia Chronicle 1847-1871: Gold & colonists*. Vancouver, BC: Discovery Press, 1977.

Audain, James. *From Coalmine to Castle*. New York: Pageant Press, 1955.

Barnes, Fred C. (ed.). *Only In Oak Bay: Oak Bay Municipality 1906-1981*. Victoria, BC: The Corporation of the District of Oak Bay, 1981.

Barr, Jennifer Nell. *Saanich Heritage Structures: An inventory*. Victoria, BC: Corporation of the District of Saanich, 1991.

Baskerville, Peter A. *Beyond the Island: An illustrated history of Victoria*. Burlington, Ontario: Windsor Publications Ltd., 1986.

Bell, Betty. *The Fair Land: Saanich*. Victoria, BC: Sono Nis Press, 1982.

British Columbia From The Earliest Times To The Present, Biographical Vol. IV. The S.J. Clarke Publishing Company, Vancouver, Portland, San Francisco, Chicago. 1914.

Camas Historical Group. *Camas Chronicles of James Bay*. Victoria, BC: Evergreen Press, Victoria, 1978.

Castle, Geoffrey (ed.). *Saanich: An illustrated history*. Sidney, BC: Manning Press, 1989.

City of Victoria. *Downtown Heritage Registry*. Victoria, BC: Corporation of the City of Victoria, 1996.

Downs, Art (ed.). *Pioneer Days in British Columbia*, Vol. 2. Surrey, BC: Heritage House, 1975.

Duffus, Maureen (ed.). *Craigflower Country: A history of View Royal 1850-1950*. Victoria, BC: Desktop Publishing Ltd., 1993.

——— (ed.). *Beyond The Blue Bridge: Stories from Esquimalt, history and reminiscences*, compiled by The Esquimalt Silver Threads Writers Group. Victoria, BC: Desktop Publishing Ltd., 1990.

Ellis, John, with Charles Lillard. *The Fernwood Files*. Victoria, BC: Orca Book Publishers, 1989.

Ewert, Henry. *The Story of the B.C. Electric Railway Company*. North Vancouver, BC: Whitecap Books, 1986.

Fawcett, Edgar. *Some Reminiscences of Old Victoria*. Toronto: William Briggs, 1912.

Grant, Peter. *The Story of Sidney*. Victoria, BC: Porthole Press, 1998.

———. *Victoria: A history in photographs.* Canmore, Aberta: Altitude Publishing Canada Ltd., 1995.

Green, Valerie. *Above Stairs: Social life in upper-class Victoria 1843-1918.* Victoria, BC: Sono Nis Press, 1995.

Hearn, G. and D. Wilkie. *The Cordwood Limited: A history of the Victoria & Sidney Railway* (revised 5th ed.). Victoria, BC: British Columbia Railway Historical Association, 1976.

Higgins, David Williams. *Tales of a Pioneer Journalist: From Gold Rush to Government Street in 19th century Victoria,* edited by Art Downs. Surrey, BC: Heritage House, 1996.

Horth, Nell. *North Saanich: Memories and pioneers.* Sidney, BC: Porthole Press,1988.

Humphreys, Danda. *On The Street Where You Live: Pioneer pathways of early Victoria.* Surrey, BC: Heritage House, 1999.

Jupp, Ursula. *From Cordwood to Campus in Gordon Head 1852-1959.* Victoria, BC: Ursula Jupp, 1975.

Kluckner, Michael. *Victoria: The Way It Was.* North Vancouver, BC: Whitecap Books, 1986.

Lindo, Millicent A. (ed.). *Making History: An anthology of British Columbia.* Victoria, BC: Millicent Lindo (publisher), 1974.

Muralt, Darryl E. *The Victoria and Sidney Railway, 1892-1919.* Victoria, BC: B.C. Railway Historical Association, 1992.

Ormsby, Margaret A. *British Columbia: A history.* Toronto: The Macmillan Company of Canada Ltd., 1958.

Pearson, Anne. *Sea–Lake: Recollections and History of Cordova Bay and Elk Lake.* Victoria, BC: Sea–Lake Editions, 1981.

Peers, Elida. *The Sooke Story: The history and the heartbeat.* Sooke, BC: Sooke Region Museum, 1999.

Pugh, Lorna Thomson. *Brentwood Bay and Me, 1930-1940: A brief history of Brentwood Bay.* Victoria, BC: Saanich Pioneers Society Archives Publications, 1997.

Reksten, Terry. *Craigdarroch: The story of Dunsmuir Castle.* Victoria, BC: Orca Book Publishers, 1987.

———. *The Dunsmuir Saga.* Vancouver, BC: Douglas & McIntyre, 1991.

Robinson, Leigh Burpee. *Esquimalt: "Place of Shoaling Waters."* Victoria, BC: Quality Press, 1947.

Robinson, Sherri K. *Esquimalt Streets and Roads: A history.* Victoria, BC: Sherri K. Robinson, 1995.

Segger, Martin & Douglas Franklin. *Exploring Victoria's Architecture.* Victoria, BC: Sono Nis Press, 1996.

Smith, Dorothy Blakey (ed.). *The Reminiscences of Doctor John Sebastian Helmcken.* Vancouver: UBC Press, 1975.

This Old House: An Inventory of Residential Heritage. Victoria, BC: City of Victoria, 1979.

Turner, Robert D. *Vancouver Island Railroads.* San Marino, California: Golden West Books, 1973.

Virgin, Victor E. *History of North and South Saanich Pioneers and District* (4th ed.). Victoria, BC: Saanich Pioneers Society, 1997.

Walbran, John T. *British Columbia Coast Names 1592-1906: Their origin and history.* North Vancouver, BC: J. J. Douglas Ltd., 1971.

Ward, Robin. *Echoes of Empire: Victoria & its remarkable buildings.* Madeira Park, BC: Harbour Publishing, 1996.

Newspapers
Victoria Times Colonist
The News Group

INDEX

PHOTO CREDITS

BC Archives: A-04656 (p. 8), A-03014 (p. 9), A-08818 (p. 10), D-07224 (p. 13, b), H-03767 (p. 13, t), H-03766 (p. 14), E-00698 (p. 17), A-01332 (p. 19, l), G-01057 (p. 19, r), A-03021 (p. 20), A-02771 (p. 21), A-01885 (p. 23), C-06134 (p. 24), A-04113 (p. 25), A-02367 (p. 27), B-05263 (p. 28), B-01505 (p. 32), C-09584 (p. 33), D-03912 (p. 37), A-02464 (p. 38, l), H-00707 (p. 38, r), C-07345 (p. 39), A-03042 (p. 40, b), C-09706 (p. 40, t), F-05340 (p. 42), C-00233 (p. 43), A-08844 (p. 44), A-04498 (p. 45), A-01219 (p. 47, l), F-03617 (p. 47, m), F-04451 (p. 47, r), I-61065 (p. 48, l), C-07427 (p. 48, l), F-08386 (p. 48, m), HP54856 (p. 48,r), G-04346 (p. 49, b), A-07630 (p. 49, t), E-01894 (p. 50), G-02071 (p. 52, l), I-61066 (p. 52, r), C-00390 (p. 53, bl), C-00391 (p. 53, br), G-09306 (p. 53, t), PDP-02900 (p. 54), A-01257 (p. 55, l), A-01253 (p. 55, r), A-02123 (p. 56), B-06365 (p. 56), D-03604 (p. 58), E-01245 (p. 60), B-02288 (p. 61), G-07025 (p. 62), B-02292 (p. 63), I-21075 (p. 64), I-51864 (p. 65), A-01460 (p. 66, l), A-01461 (p. 66, r), D-00256 (p. 67), G-04888 (p. 68), A-04630 (p. 69), E-09075 (p. 71), B-02246 (p. 72), C-06701 (p. 73), E-09109 (p. 74, b), E-02696 (p. 74, t), G-00154 (p. 75), G-05954 (p. 76, l), A-02716 (p. 77), A-03010 (p. 79), C-09496 (p. 80, l), C-09497 (p. 80, r), PDP 03811 (p. 81), A-03407 (p. 83), F-07390 (p. 84, l), F-02849 (p. 84, r), F-05386 (p. 86, b), F-06587 (p. 86, t), A-01737 (p. 87), D-00389 (p. 88, l), A-01389 (p. 88, r), E-00495 (p. 92), H-06831 (p. 93, l), I-00954 (p. 93, r), G-05244 (p. 96), I-46844 (p. 96), B-04323 (p. 97), A-03005 (p. 98), E-09110 (p. 100, l), A-01222 (p. 100, r), B-09628 (p. 101), D-05693 (p. 102), C-03679 (p. 103, b), G-02903 (p. 103, t), G-05567 (p. 105), E-02771 (p. 108), G-02905 (p. 109), PDP 06552 (p. 111), C-03757 (p. 112, t), G-06774 (p. 113, tl), G-05492 (p. 113, tr), A-01695 (p. 115, b), F-04208 (p. 115, t), D-03954 (p. 116), C-06405 (p. 117), D-05607 (p. 119), D-05614 (p. 120), D-05609 (p. 121, b), C-07039 (p. 121, t), E-04561 (p. 122), I-00078 (p. 124), F-02386 (p. 125, b), D-08870 (p. 125, m), F-02389 (p. 125, t), D-06362 (p. 128, b), B-03703 (p. 128, t; front cover), B-01680 (p. 131), G-03772 (p. 133), G-06272 (p. 136, r), H-03410 (p. 137), A-02124 (p. 139), A-08906 (p. 140), C-03835 (p. 144, b), A-04402 (p. 144, t), B-04309 (p. 146), G-02915 (p. 149), A-01226 (p. 150), B-04311 (p. 151, b), B-04310 (p. 151, t), G-02906 (p. 152, b), B-08068 (p. 152, t), A-06621 (p. 154), D-00513 (p. 155, t), D-05673) (p. 157), D-06835 (p. 158, l), D-06832 (p. 158, r), B-01959 (p. 159, t), H-00665 (p. 162), F-09890 (p. 164), D-04035 (p. 166), D-04032 (p. 167, t), I-61064 (p. 169), I-61064 (p. 169), D-03639 (p. 173), C-07550 (p. 174), E-02446 (p. 177) PDP02611 (back cover, t), PDP01208 (back cover, b), I-51686 (front cover flap, t) PDP04463 (front cover flap, b).

Saanich Archives: 29997 (p. 18), 28554 (p. 104), 1981-7-33 (p. 130), 1980-10-36 (p. 136, t), 1985-8-9A (p. 138), 1993-1-4 (p. 145, b), 1993-1-11 (p. 145, t), 1978-1-3 (p. 148), 1985-6-45 (p. 155), 1981-19-6 (p. 156), 1981-19-97 (p. 163), 1981-1-1 (p. 169, b), 1980-8-1 (p. 169, t), 1980-8-11 (p. 170), 1978-1-53 (p. 171).

Sidney Museum: P981.004 (p. 165).

Sooke Region Historical Society: 459 (p. 175).

Victoria City Archives: 96604-01-2759 (p. 30), 96604-01-2754 (p. 35), 98601-25-1390 (p. 36), PR104-3397 (p. 70, l), PR104-3423) (P. 70, r), PR252-7532 (p. 76, r), 98702-02-2135 (p. 78), PR37-7479 (p. 82), PRPD99-7544 (p. 85), PR234-1654 (p. 89), 96604-01-4065 (p. 94), 99008-01-3495 (p. 95), 97903-01-4833 (p. 113, b), PR88-414 (p. 126), 96609-01-6577 (p. 129), 96609-01-6593 (p. 132), 98410-10-635 (p. 134), PR73-5915 (p. 141, l), PR73-6129 (p. 141, r), 96609-01-6586 (p. 142), PR88-618 (p. 159, b), 98610-17-2127 (p. 160).

Robin Clarke: author photo (back cover flap and p. 188).

Heritage House Collection: (p. 90).

Lorna Thomson Pugh Collection: (p. 153).

The map on page 106 is based on a *Times Colonist* map produced by Rob Struthers.

THE AUTHOR

"Victoria's Favourite Street Walker"

Originally from Cheshire, England, Danda has lived in Canada since 1972 and on the West Coast since 1982. She arrived in Victoria in late 1996 and quickly noticed that many of its street names were different from those in other Canadian cities. At each intersection she paused and pondered. Then, realizing she was getting a reputation for standing on street corners, Danda "went underground," to libraries, archives, and pioneer societies. She wrote three articles about the origin of Victoria's street names ... and a newspaper series was born.

Danda's habit of ambling along every street she features, in order to absorb its atmosphere, has earned her the unofficial title of "Victoria's Favourite Street Walker." She is often joined in her meanderings by local residents and visitors, who are also fascinated by the colourful characters who once walked the streets of this city. Danda's special storytelling ability is enjoyed by all those who "Step Back In Time" on her guided tours of Victoria's historic downtown, hop on one of her open-top bus tours, gather for spooky stories in a cemetery, watch her on TV, or listen to her on the radio.

Danda's weekly column on the history of street names first appeared in the Victoria *Times Colonist*'s "Islander" magazine in October 1997. In 1999 her first book (pictured left) became one of the city's fastest selling regional titles in the past two decades. This is her second book about Victoria's nineteenth-century pioneers. She is currently researching a third.

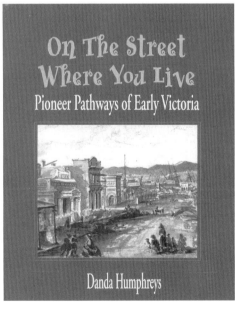

On The Street Where You Live
Pioneer Pathways of Early Victoria

Danda Humphreys

ISBN 1-895811-90-2 $34.95
Available from your favourite bookseller
or Heritage House (www.heritagehouse.ca)